Stock Market Crashes

International Bestsellers by Ravi Batra

The Downfall of Capitalism and Communism, Macmillan, London, 1978, and Tokuma, Tokyo, 1995

The Great Depression of 1990, Simon & Schuster, New York, 1987

Surviving The Great Depression of 1990, Simon & Schuster, New York, 1988

The Myth of Free Trade, Macmillan, New York, 1993, and Kobansha, Tokyo, 1994

Ravi Batra's Forecasts, Sogo Horei, Tokyo, 1995

Other Books by Ravi Batra

The Great American Deception, John Wiley & Sons, New York, 1996

Japan: The Return to Prosperity, Sogo Horei, Tokyo, 1996

Studies In The Pure Theory Of International Trade, St. Martin Press, New York, 1972

The Pure Theory Of International Trade Under Uncertainty, New York, Wiley Inter Science, 1976

Stock Market Crashes
of
1998 and 1999

Ravi Batra

Liberty Press
care of Venus Books
2355 Trellis Place
Richardson, TX. 75081

Hang Tough in Adversity
Tomorrow Will Surely
Come A Golden Age

In the memory of my late teacher
Shri Prabhat Ranjan Sarkar

Contents

Chapters

Preface

On page 174 of my latest work, *The Great American Deception*, I predicted that there would be a stock market crash by the end of 1997. I have made similar forecasts in my lectures and books printed in Japan. Now that share prices have indeed crashed or suffered a serious decline in many parts of the world, it is time to write a brief treatise about the future performance of stock exchanges.

At the beginning of October, share prices began to collapse in the economies of the Asian tigers. By the end of the month, the rout was on, and afflicted many nations in the final week. History was made on October 27, 1997, that fateful day known as Manic Monday, when trading was halted twice on the New York Stock Exchange, with the Dow Jones Index plummeting a record 554 points. In percentage terms, the Dow fell only 7.2%, and recovered much of the fall through a record rise of 337 points the next day. Nevertheless, US share markets had been shaken, while markets in Latin America and Asia were in turmoil.

I believe bigger market jolts are yet to come not just in Asia and South America but in Europe and the United States as well. In fact, another global jolt is likely in the first quarter of 1998, if not sooner. Here is why. The fundamental economic force underlying national and global economies is the force of supply and demand. Supply springs from production or labor productivity, and demand from wages. Since 1990, thanks to globalization and the recession that year, wages have lagged behind productivity all over the world. If productivity rises but wages stagnate, supply grows faster than demand and an imbalance begins to develop.

For a while the supply-demand gap can be plugged by bank loans and consumer debt, and consumer demand can be artificially lifted to match the rising supply. In the meanwhile profits rise sharply as wages fail to grow, thereby creating a hefty rise in stock prices. In fact, the bigger the gap between productivity and wages, the bigger the rise in profits and stock prices, and hence the bigger the eventual trouble. There comes a point when banks stop lending or debt-burdened consumers reduce their borrowing. Then the supply-demand gap surfaces.

This critical point arrived in July 1997 in the tiger economies of South East Asia, where banks have sharply curtailed their lending. The United States has also indirectly suffered in the process. In the US, the lending continues, but consumer debt is at an all-time high and personal bankruptcies are soaring. For this, as well as other reasons I am about to discuss, the supply-demand gap will soon reach American shores.

Since Summer 1997, Thailand, Malaysia, Singapore, Taiwan and Indonesia have experienced major currency depreciations relative to the dollar. Similarly, the yen has also lost 50% of its value since late 1995. All this tends to make US exports expensive abroad and Asian imports cheaper at home. Therefore, we will see exports fall and imports rise, in a similar process that occurred in the aftermath of the Mexican peso crisis in 1995. The resultant ballooning of the US trade deficit will further crimp demand for American goods, causing a fall in the profits of American companies.

Some US multinationals will indeed benefit from cheaper goods produced abroad, but their gain will be a small fraction of sales losses suffered by American companies as a result of the mushrooming deficit. All in all, American companies will see mild to major declines in their profitability. Stock prices represented by the Dow have risen from a low of 800 in 1982 to over 7500 by the end of October 1997, all from the promise of ever-rising profitability of American corporations. When profits decline, even the most die-hard of American investors will run for cover. Share prices will then crash in America.

The bullish case for American shares, in spite of the current turmoil in Asian and Latin American markets, comes mostly from Wall Street brokers. They ask us to look at the current fundamentals such as low inflation, low interest rates and low unemployment. But they overlook 1929, when inflation, interest rates and unemployment were even lower, and yet such "sound" fundamentals did not prevent the market collapse and the Great Depression. The only fundamental that really counts is the one we learn in any college course on economic principles, namely supply and demand. And that is where a serious gap has now emerged in the global economy.

The book has a total of seven chapters, in which you will discover the historical background behind the currently growing crisis, and where the crisis is going to take us. The first chapter argues that America today has a global business empire that, in many ways, resembles the Roman colonial empire. In the second chapter, we take a close look at the Asian tigers, and why they are in turmoil.

Next, we turn to the economic illness of Japan, whose vast industrial accomplishments since 1950 have faded somewhat in the 1990s. Chapters 4 and 5 analyze global speculative bubbles, and why they began crashing in the middle of 1997. Chapter 6 presents a vision of the near future, when the US business empire is likely to fall. It describes how the global financial markets in stocks, bonds currencies, real estate, gold and other assets are likely to behave in 1998 and 1999. Once you know how these markets are going to react, you can protect your assets from serious losses that many will face. Despite the current atmosphere of gloom and doom in Asia, the future is very bright for us all. But we will have to work very hard to escape today's turmoil, and to achieve tomorrow's brilliance. In this spirit, the 7th and last chapter is devoted to economic reform, which we cannot afford to ignore to create a better world for our children.

In finishing this project, I gratefully acknowledge the help I have received from my friends, Amitabh Singh, Arvind Chaudhary, Bernie Ingaso, Thor Thorgeirsson, Walt Bunjee, Kamal Saggi, Darwin Payne, Spencer Mcgowan, and my dear wife, Sunita. Thanks are also due to Tachibana for deciding to speed up the publication of the book in Japan. The contribution of every one at Tachibana is invaluable, because without their tireless efforts, the information contained in these pages would not have reached the Japanese readers in time for them to take proper defensive action. Last, but not least, I am thankful to Morgan Stanley Capital International for allowing me to use its data underlying some figures.

Ravi Batra
Dallas, December 12, 1997

* * *

1. The American Business

Empire

Normally when we talk about an empire, we think of the British empire or the Roman empire among many others. We think of colonies, captured territories, and conquered people. We speak of long battles among the nations that fight for supremacy over the seas, earth and skies. In short, we think about enslaved areas inside the boundaries of a colonial empire. But what about a business empire?

A national business empire may appear to be totally different from a colonial empire, but in reality it has many similarities. Although it does not have political dominance over other nations, it has commercial dominance. In the case of the colonial empire, the victorious country has the highest living standard; it collects gifts and taxes from the conquered people; its ideas, values, language and culture spread to captured areas;

it obtains cheap labor from the people under its dominance; and above all, it has military supremacy over imperial territories. In all these respects, the American business empire of today has the features of a colonial empire.

At this point you wonder: Does America really have a business empire today? In other words, does American business have political dominance inside the United States and commercial dominance in some parts of the world? Yes. In fact, you will find that in terms of business interests, America today has control over the biggest empire ever amassed in the world.

The Roman Empire

Let us begin with Rome. Some two thousand years ago, around 30 BC, the Romans built a powerful army, conquered the city states, then defeated many nations, and in the process created a vast empire that stretched from western Europe to north Africa and west Asia. The victors extracted gifts, taxes and slaves from the defeated people. This gave the Romans the highest living standard inside their empire. Their language, culture, ideas and values spread throughout their territories.

Rome did it all with the force of arms. Before the powerful Roman army, no neighboring city and nation was safe. The defeated people built a rich economy for the victors. The standard of living in Rome was almost as high as in some advanced nations today. As a respected historian, M. Rostovtzeff says, "One can say without exaggeration that never in the history of mankind (except during the 19th and 20th centuries in Europe and America) has a large number of people enjoyed so much comfort; and that never, not even in the 19th century, did men live in such a surrounding of beautiful buildings and monuments as in the first two centuries of the Roman Empire." (p. 291)

18

These are incredible words, but they have come from an eminent scholar, who has been well recognized for his contributions to the history of Rome. The Roman economy was built by new technology, capital accumulation and cheap labor obtained from slaves captured from the colonies. The slaves worked in farms, factories and homes in exchange for food, clothing and shelter. In other words, they worked for a minimum and just subsistence wage.

The Roman empire was the first warrior age in western history following the birth of the Christian prophet, Jesus Christ. In this age, the army dominates most, if not all, social institutions. That is why it should not be surprising that army officers had the highest prestige and living standard in Rome. They owned the best homes, slaves and comforts. A career in the army was eagerly sought, because that was a sure way to obtain the amenities of life.

Rome was the cultural and commercial center of the empire, especially in the first two centuries. People from imperial provinces wished to emigrate to that city and become Roman citizens. To that end they were ready to do anything, even work voluntarily as slaves. Thus, slave labor, forced as well as unforced, built a rich Roman economy that included prosperous sectors in agriculture, manufacturing and commerce.

The empire had flourishing trade with the colonies as well as the neighboring empires of India, Persia and China. Major industries included pottery, textiles, metal and glass. These industries provided goods for export, while imports consisted mainly of spices, silk and jewelry.

The development of crop rotation and soil fertilization led to a flourishing agriculture, which, of course, was also aided by slave labor. Yet, in spite of great overall prosperity, the economy was far from perfect even in the first two centuries of the empire, because high salaries and wealth were confined to the upper classes, especially the military.

In general, people disliked physical work, which was reserved for the slaves, whose supply fell with the passage of time. The falling supply of manual labor, in turn, resulted in production declines in most industries. In addition, Italy ran a persistent trade deficit with its provinces that included the subject nations. The deficits were partly financed by taxes collected from the provinces and partly by the export of precious metals that drained the nation of gold and silver. Rome suffered a great economic decline, especially in the third century after the creation of the empire, and finally it led to the fall of the imperial government in 476 AD

There are two main reasons for the fall of Rome. One, as already noted, was the economic decline; the other was extreme militarism. In order to maintain peace in the colonies, the government had to maintain a vast army and navy. There was, no doubt, a long period of peace in the first two centuries of the empire, but it exacted a heavy price. The government had to impose huge taxes, which fell mostly on farmers and businesses in the provinces, and to some extent on those in Italy. Such heavy taxation and the collection efforts resulted in a vast bureaucracy, government waste and production declines. Thus large military expenditures and the ultimate loss of prosperity were linked to each other.

Although Roman society vanished a long time ago, some of its contributions have survived till this day. Rome's main gift to humanity was and is its concept of law, which held that all people are equal; that everyone is entitled to certain rights that the government cannot violate, and every person is innocent until proven guilty. This is the concept of natural law that in theory was even above the state. Although, in reality, the elites, then as now, received preferential treatment and justice, this legal concept is prevalent in western society even today. Indeed, it is the foundation of all democracies.

* * *

The British Empire

The last great kingdom of the world was the British empire, which included overseas territories ruled by a small European island called Britain. Unlike Rome, Britain built its empire through commercial interests, especially its East India Company, which secured a base in India in the late 17th century. By the middle of the 18th century, Britain had established colonies in the Caribbean, North America and India.

Britain lost its 13 American colonies in the American revolution of 1776, but renewed its territorial expansion in the 19th century. It then established control over areas in South East Asia, Australia and Africa. By World War I, the empire extended over one-fourth of the world population and land.

Although the empire was started by commercial interests, which had their own militias, the British military's control over the colonies was as absolute as that of Rome over its provinces. Inside England, parliamentary democracy began with the Glorious Revolution in 1689, and steadily evolved in the 18th and 19th centuries, but in most territories British governors and army officers ruled with an iron hand. The citizens of subject nations were not treated as slaves, but they were not allowed any rights.

Early in the 20th century, Britain permitted self government in some territories such as India and Australia; but the colonies remained dissatisfied with restrained self rule. They did have elections and legislative assemblies, but their powers were limited to matters of local concern. India, in fact, erupted into a full-blown mass movement against the foreign rule, and finally gained independence in 1947. Earlier, in 1942, Britain had granted complete autonomy to Australia, and other colonies were gradually freed after 1947. By 1960, the empire had all but disappeared. What is remarkable is that most of the colonies gained freedom in a peaceful way, for the first time in history.

Britain exploited its territories in a variety of ways. As usual, the colonies benefited the imperial nation and helped raise its living standard. Britain encouraged the policy of free trade inside the territories, but imposed tariffs on manufactured imports from them. Thus, the colonies supplied cheap raw materials for protected British manufactures, in which England had an early lead because of its industrial revolution. Nevertheless, the country discouraged manufacturing imports from subject nations by imposing tariffs on such products; but raw materials were kept free from import duties.

The colonies, of course, were not permitted to impose tariffs on their manufactured imports. This way, the colonies provided cheap raw materials and markets for British industry, which grew manifold. Industries such as textiles, machine tools, iron, ship-building among many others grew apace, but colonial industries were destroyed by mass-produced goods coming from Britain.

The captured territories also ran trade surpluses to pay for services imported from Britain at highly inflated prices. British governors and civil and army officers worked in the colonies at high salaries, which were in turn financed by excess foreign exchange reserves earned with surplus trade with England. This way the British economic policy worked to the sole benefit of the English people at the expense of subject nations.

Unlike Rome, Britain did not force its subjects into slavery, but it did obtain cheap labor from them in another way. The territories were used to recruit soldiers, who, while receiving subsistence wages, fought for Britain to defend its colonies in the two world wars. Thus the British army benefited from cheap labor and freed the resources for Britain's own economic development.

However, the monopoly over colonial labor and product markets left British industry vulnerable to competition from other advanced economies. British firms were not as efficient as the firms in Germany and the United States. Therefore, after the dissolution of the empire, Britain suffered a rapid economic decline at least relative to other developed countries. The nation suffered from inflation, labor unrest, trade deficits and a steady decline of its currency.

There is no doubt that Britain heavily exploited its colonies for national economic gain; but it also made useful contributions to their social structure. It introduced them to democratic institutions, modern technology and some degree of industrialization. Democracy was alien to India before it was conquered by the East India Company. But Indian intellectuals studying in England learned English, the British law and the concept of parliamentary rule. As a result, after independence India did not revert to monarchy and dictatorship that had been the rule prior to its annexation into the empire.

The British also succeeded in freeing Indians of some of their most heinous social practices. For instance, centuries old practice of Sati, in which widows were burned alive along with their dead husbands, was outlawed. The British law, language and culture are thriving in their former colonies even today.

The US Business Empire

The term business empire normally makes us think of extremely rich people. Billionaires are commonly said to own wealthy and large corporations spread across the globe. A business empire thus is generally associated with affluent people or an affluent group of people. The term is rarely, if ever, used for a nation. In what sense, then, does the United States have a business empire?

A brief description of the two colonial empires, one modern and the other ancient, reveals four common features.

First, the empire is created through the force of arms either by military officers or by commercial interests. Second, the ruling nation obtains cheap labor from its colonies. Third, the colonies run trade surpluses that raise the living standard or the consumption levels of their rulers. Finally, the language and culture of the victors spread across the colonies.

Of the four features just listed, three apply to the US influence around the world today. The United States does not seek to conquer other nations, although it is militarily strong enough to do so. Yet its economic policies and multinational corporations have enabled it to enjoy benefits that in the past accrued only to imperial powers.

Following the Second World War, America pursued an economic policy of free trade and investment. This policy has won the nation privileges that it could not secure at the battle field. In the Korean war, China and North Korea held America to a draw, as the results of the war were inconclusive. In the Vietnam war, the United States suffered a crushing defeat in spite of overwhelming military superiority. But what the US failed to win militarily, it won through its economic and business policies.

Today, both China and Vietnam seek expanded commerce with the United States. China, in fact, has become dependent on its US trade, and the United States, as discussed later, is increasingly dependent on Chinese holdings of American government bonds. America does not dominate other nations politically, but it dominates them commercially. In this respect, the dominance is far more pervasive than that of colonial empires. For the military conquests in the past rarely encompassed more than one fourth of the world's land and population, but the US business and cultural influence now spans over virtually the entire planet.

The fall of the Berlin Wall in 1989 and the subsequent fall of Soviet communism left the United States as the world's sole super power. Immediately after World War II, nations were divided into three blocs, namely the American bloc, the Soviet bloc and a group of non-aligned nations. The capitalist United States and the communist Soviet Union competed vigorously for influence in non-aligned countries.

Even though America gave them a great deal of financial aid, many non-aligned nations feared and respected the dictatorial Soviet Union and its vast army equipped with nuclear weapons. In many Third World nations, the communist ideology was more popular than capitalist thought. Even in western Europe, leftist parties occasionally won elections because of their proximity with the Soviet System. Thus although the Soviet Union could not match the United States economically, its dictatorial political system that inspired fearful respect at home and abroad enabled it to have greater influence in the Third World.

All this, however, changed abruptly after the disintegration of the Soviet empire in the early 1990s. Russian influence waned in the Soviet satellites of Poland, Hungary, East Germany, Czechoslovakia and Romania, while some of its former provinces such as Ukraine, Georgia, and Azerbaijan seceded from the Soviet confederation. As a result, after 1991 Russia suffered an economic depression, which is still not over.

With Russia in a free economic fall and preoccupied with internal political instability, the United States is now the foremost military power in the world. Prior to the Cold War, the Soviet Union almost always denounced US economic and foreign policies. There was very little cooperation between them. But now Russia needs financial aid from the West to stabilize and develop its economy. It rarely opposes US foreign policy initiatives, leaving America the predominant military power in the world.

In the Gulf War of 1991, for instance, the United States, leading its allies, invaded Iraq, while Russia looked the other way. In the prior days of the Cold War, however, this would not have happened, no matter how hard the world screamed against Iraq's invasion of Kuwait. The United States responded with force to bring down the price of oil. In fact, the Soviet Union, an oil exporter and thus a beneficiary of a high oil price, would have aligned itself with Iraq, and that would have been enough to keep America at bay. But things are different now. The main restraint on the US military right now is the American public which would not permit an unfair use of armed forces to extract concessions from other countries.

Within a colonial empire, the ruling nation has the strongest army. America today does not own colonies, but its armed forces are the strongest in the world. This gives the country a level of political influence that others lack. At the very least, the US political impact on other nations and at the United Nations exceeds that of any other country. Does this mean that America has an empire? Perhaps not. But it is a factor that should be kept in mind, while examining the totality of American global influence.

The second feature of a national empire is that the ruling state obtains cheap labor from its colonies. This feature certainly applies to the United States today. America obtains cheap labor in two ways. Immigration to the country, legal and illegal, expands the US labor supply, thereby restraining domestic wages. Illegal immigrants coming mostly from Mexico and Latin America work for subsistence wages. But for their influx, US wages would be much higher. It should be mentioned here that immigration to America is voluntary and eagerly sought, for the country is the land of riches and freedom.

Secondly American multinationals employ thousands of workers in Latin America, Asia and Africa, paying local wages that are just a fraction of domestic wages. Products made by this labor force that includes children are then imported into the United States, further depressing US wages. However, this practice generates high profits for the multinationals and exceptionally high incomes for their managers.

Here again the United States gets these benefits voluntarily without the force of arms, but the benefits are there and are substantial for the business elites. Businessmen are the richest people in America. Their income and wealth have sky-rocketed since 1980, while the incomes of others have been stagnant. Their tax burden has declined while that of the poor and the middle class has risen significantly. Thus in the US business empire, as in colonial empires of the past, cheap labor from abroad provides great benefits to the elites.

The third, and perhaps the most interesting feature, of an empire is that the ruler forces trade surpluses on its colonies, while running trade deficits itself to raise its level of consumption. Likewise, the United States has enjoyed a high level of trade deficit with the world since 1983 without firing a single bullet.

In the ancient past, Rome obtained some goods free from its provinces by imposing heavy taxes on them, as the collected revenue financed a part of its trade deficit. Britain also obtained goods freely from its territories by forcing them to pay for administrative services provided by its citizens at inflated prices. Now the United States obtains some products from the world at no cost. How is this possible?

The greenback is the single most-acceptable currency in the world, which needs increasing amounts of dollars to finance growing trade. A country's money is called a key currency, if it is globally acceptable to carry out commerce. The dollar is a key currency, so are the yen, the pound and the Deutsche mark. But the dollar is the most acceptable of all key currencies.

The world does not want to hoard pounds, marks and yens, but it has been hoarding dollars since 1983. In other words, America pays for its import surplus, the excess of imports over exports, through paper dollars, and its only visible cost is the cost of printing dollar bills, especially the large denomination

100-dollar notes, which the world seems to love. More of these bills circulate elsewhere than in the United States itself.

Why the world is happy to accept paper money in exchange for solid goods will be discussed later. For now it may be noted that America has had a persistent import surplus with the rest of the world in the 1980s and the 1990s at practically no cost.

Never before in history has a nation run an enduring trade deficit with free nations without exporting silver and gold. But America has somehow managed to do so. To be sure, the country also had a persistent import surplus in the 19th century, but at that time, Europeans lent money for American investment projects and thus financed excessive imports. Now it does not seem to matter. The world obtains paper dollars and then invests them in American stock and bond markets. The commercial process is now reversed.

In the past, a country would borrow money from abroad and then pay for its trade deficit; thus the deficit was limited by the borrowing. But now America simply imports as much as it wants, and the world pockets the dollars. Of course, other countries are still subject to the old-fashioned discipline.

Even other key-currency countries such as Britain, Japan and Germany cannot afford to run persistent import surpluses without suffering currency depreciations or rising interest rates needed to attract foreign investors in their bonds. But the United States is one country today with a hefty trade deficit and a strong currency — all fruits of its business empire. The trade deficit produces an interesting comparison about the standard of living in different countries.

Per capita GDP(gross domestic product) is normally used as a measure of inter-country living standards. In this measure, the United States lags behind Switzerland and Germany. But when we compare per-capita levels of consumption, America comes first. This is because, total consumption equals GDP plus the trade deficit, or GDP minus the trade surplus. Clearly,

Americans are great beneficiaries of their empire today. How long will all this last, we shall study in chapter 6.

The fourth and final feature of an empire concerns the spread of the ruler's language, customs and culture across the imperial territories. In this respect also, the United States enjoys the same privilege. English is the language of the elites in most countries. For this Britain deserves as much credit as the United States. Fiction and non-fiction books published by US presses are the most popular around the world. They are avidly sought by young people, who love America's pop culture and music. The United States is the largest exporter of films and TV shows.

Teenagers around the globe know more about American movie stars then their own political leaders. Fast food from the likes of McDonald's is not just an American craze; it is now becoming a worldwide craze. American materialism is also fast infecting the world's youth. Foreign TV shows and movies now display the same type of sex and violence that is popular on US entertainment shows.

Thanks to the US influence, capitalism has spread all over the world. Soviet communism and its ideology are there no more; similarly, China is fast adopting American production techniques and methods. Most of its state enterprises are being dismantled or privatized to make them efficient. Today Chinese economic communism exists, but it is fast evolving into a new type of production system.

It is no exaggeration to say that the American global influence has been at its zenith in the 1990s, towering even above its world status following the Second World War. In that war, much of the world was annihilated, while the US economy emerged unchallenged and unscathed. American industry had practically no competitors. Yet, the ideology of capitalism was contested by the leftist philosophy. Soviet communism did not have much to show for success, but it had millions of believers.

The Soviet war alliance with America until 1946 and the subsequent Chinese revolution in 1949 combined to give communism an aura of moral superiority over capitalism. Capitalism appeared to be for the rich, communism for the masses. Former enemies — Russia, China, Vietnam — now seek expanded economic ties with the United States.

Moreover, the United States had an enduring trade surplus after the war. A major feature of an empire is that the ruler obtains free gifts of goods and services from the colonies through its trade deficit. The US enjoys that privilege today and has ever since 1983.

Multinational Corporations

Many countries, including developing ones like India and Mexico, have multinational corporations today. But US multinationals are in a class of their own. Their top managers, called CEO's or chief executive officers, have the highest salaries in the world. Japan, Germany, France and England also have many global corporations, but their managers earn about a third of US managers.

Business privileges in America are simply outlandish. Even when some CEOs are fired, they get a huge package of benefits. One corporation fired its top officer for incompetence in 1996, but rewarded him with $90 million in severance pay. Another corporation gave $300 million to an officer's estate to be paid after death.

Big business in America, as in other democracies, owns politicians. In fact, both political parties, Democrats and Republicans, are beholden to the wealthy. In congressional and presidential elections in 1996, nearly two billion dollars were spent. Of course, those who provide money reap rich rewards for their investment. In some cases, their rate of return is 100 times their donation; that is, for one dollar

30

offered to a politician, they receive $100 in tax benefits or governmental business contracts.

Business elites in America are like the Roman generals of the past, dominating the economy, society and politics. Money controls US politics as never before. As a result, the tax burden has been gradually shifted from the wealthy onto the backs of the poor and the middle class. From 1950 to 1980, the top-bracket income tax rate ranged from 70 to 90 percent, while the Social Security tax imposed on lower incomes varied from 4 to 9 percent. By 1997 the top income tax rate was down to 39.6 percent, but the Social Security tax had jumped to 15.3 percent. Such are the tangible benefits that moneyed donors receive from politicians.

The transfer of the tax burden to the poor was justified in the name of promoting investment and growth. But as I demonstrated in *The Great American Deception*, the growth rate fell sharply in the 1980s and the 1990s, while the investment rate fell a little. All this happened just when businesses reaped huge rewards from their political investments.

In the 1950s, corporations used to pay 25 percent of the federal tax revenue; in 1997, their tax share was down to 10 percent. Did they put more money in investment? No. How could they? Consumer demand, under the burden of predatory taxes on the poor and the middle class, did not grow as fast as before? How can investment rise unless a business has more in sales? No one puts more money in his company, if he loses customers, even if the government gives many tax breaks. The folly of overbuilding became clear in July 1997 in Thailand, when office buildings stood empty because of a lack of consumer demand.

Income Disparity

With Big Business in complete command of the American

31

Figure 1

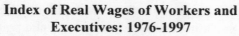

Index of Real Wages of Workers and
Executives: 1976-1997

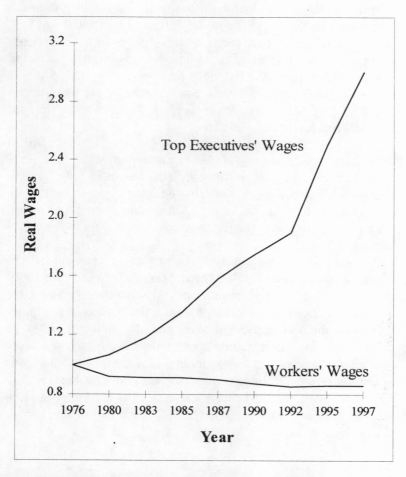

Source: Ravi Batra, *The Great American Deception;* and
New York Times

economy and some factories using cheap labor abroad, it should not come as a surprise that wages of chief executives have sky-rocketed; but what is surprising is that the real wages of workers have steadily declined in an economy where productivity continues to rise.

Consider Figure 1, which plots the real wage index of chief executives· and their employees.   The real wage is the purchasing power of a person's salary.   Both wage indexes start at one in 1976, but then the executives' index soars 175 percent by 1997, whereas that of workers falls 14% in the same period.   On top of this, workers' tax burden has also jumped while that of the executives has plunged. Is there any doubt that Big Business rules America? Not from Figure 1.

The real wages of American employees have actually been declining since 1972.   According to The Economic Report of the President, an annual publication of the federal government, weekly earnings of production workers, measured in 1982 prices, were $315 in 1972 and $260 in 1997.   This is a hefty decrease of 17%, which does not take into account the tripling of the Social Security tax and state sales taxes, both of which fall disproportionately on the poor and the middle-class.   In view of such giant tax increases, real wages of production workers, who constitute at least 75% of the labor force, have plunged by more than 25%.   No wonder, income disparity has soared. However, the inequality for wealth distribution is even worse.

Figure 2 is a portrait of wealth disparity. What is the difference between income and wealth? Income is what a person earns from work and investments.   Wealth is whatever has been saved or inherited from the past.   In the case of wealth, the disparity is even more astounding.

Figure 2 displays the trends in wealth disparity from 1929 to 1997. In 1929, the year the Great Depression began, just 1% of Americans owned 36% of national wealth; their share fell to 21% by 1949. It then began a steady climb and by

33

Figure 2

Concentration of Wealth in America
(in percent): 1929-1995

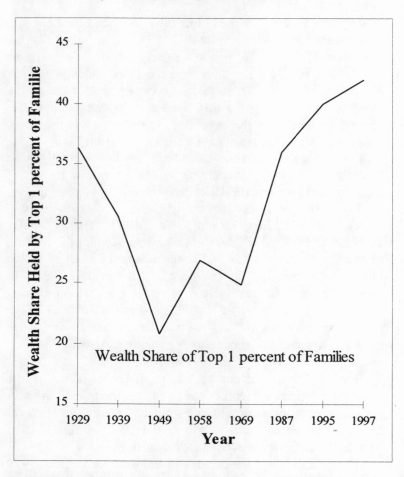

Source: Ravi Batra, *The Great American Deception;* and
         New York Times

1997, 1% of Americans had 42% of their country's total wealth.

With the American business empire expanding its reach, it is not surprising that income and wealth disparity has been rising all over the world. The spread of capitalism means rising inequality over the globe, even in China, Russia and the former Soviet satellites. Growing inequality has always ended in growing poverty and financial instability. That is why the government economic policies including taxation and spending should never promote income and wealth disparities.

Globalization of the US Economy

How did the United States manage to amass the largest business empire ever built in the world? The answer to this question will also tell us how top American executives have succeeded in collecting huge salaries and wealth.

Following World War II, the United States was the strongest economic power on earth. Its industrial might was unmatched, its technology envied and in demand all over the globe. What is interesting is that the country depended very little on foreign trade. In 1950, US exports were just 5% of GDP, whereas US imports were 4% of GDP. In the technical language of economics, the country was nearly a closed economy, not open to foreign competition.

By contrast, the war had devastated the economies of Russia, China, Japan, Germany, Italy, France and Britain. In order to contain the rising tide of communism, the United States launched what is known as the Marshall Plan as well as a policy of globalization. The idea was to enable western Europe to grow rapidly through financial aid as well as freer trade with the United States. America also helped Japan through export of technology and by opening its markets to imports. This way the United States hoped to build up its allies to counter the threat of communism from the Soviet

Union and China.

Powered by US aid and trade, western Europe and especially Japan grew apace and turned into unexpectedly strong competitors. American businessmen never foresaw the challenge that was to emerge from war ravaged nations. By 1970 the American trade surplus had turned into a trade deficit. The world was awash in dollars.

Unlike today, other nations at that time were not ready to accept American dollars indefinitely for their trade surplus. The world wanted payment in gold, which was plentiful in the United States, but not enough to finance a persistent trade deficit.

After protracted trade negotiations among G-7 countries (America, Canada, Britain, France, Germany, Italy and Japan), the link between the dollar and gold was severed in 1973, and the world moved from a fixed exchange standard to a flexible rate system. Until that year, the international price of gold was fixed at $35 per ounce, and all other currencies were linked to the dollar. The yen, for instance, was fixed at the rate of 360 to one, but in 1973 and thereafter, the dollar began to fall and the yen began to rise. The value of currencies was no longer fixed, but was determined by market forces of supply and demand.

The idea was that flexible exchange rates would eliminate trade deficits and thus the US need to export gold. In fact, this is what happened in the 1970s, and the US import surplus all but disappeared. This occurred in spite of the global turmoil caused by the rocketing price of oil.

Economic conditions changed dramatically in the 1980s. High inflation along with the need to curb it through restrained bank lending sharply raised US interest rates. Foreign money poured into the United States to earn high yields. This raised the demand for dollars and caused an appreciation of the currency. Expensive currency means expensive goods abroad and cheaper foreign goods. Consequently, US exports fell, but imports rose, and the trade deficit made a return, this time to stay forever.

What had changed the world's willingness to hold paper dollars for goods and services? The main change had occurred in Japan, where consumer demand was not growing as fast as before. In order to increase production at the old high rates, Japanese companies began to sell more and more of their products abroad, especially the United States. This generated more dollars in their hands, but at least they could keep their production growth high.

In the meantime, the US government needed to borrow large amounts of money to finance its growing budget deficit. Japanese companies and the bank of Japan used a part of their surplus dollars to buy US government bonds. Another part went into the purchase of US factories and real estate.

The reinvestment of Japan's surplus foreign exchange into American assets prevented the depreciation of the dollar, which would have normally followed the US trade deficit. This suited Japan fine, but in the process created growing dependence of the nation on foreign demand.

After 1985, the G-7 countries adopted a policy of dollar depreciation to bring the US deficit down. The dollar's value fell sharply relative to other currencies, but the deficit fell very slowly, mainly because several years of the US policy of globalization had resulted in a vast inflow of manufactured imports in American markets. In the process the domestic industrial base had shrunk.

Several sectors of production had been in retreat-- autos, consumer electronics, machine tools, textiles, shoes, etc. In spite of the dollar depreciation, the home production of goods and services was not high enough to match home demand. The difference between the two equaled the trade deficit.

Japan had experienced phenomenal growth after 1950. For 40 straight years, with few exceptions, the country kept growing at an average rate of 8% per year. It served as a model for the neighboring countries of South Korea, Taiwan, Singapore, Hong Kong and even China. They sought to emulate Japan first by creating a vast industrial base and then by exporting their goods abroad, mainly to the United States. If, in the process, they had to accept paper dollars or reinvest them in US government bonds, then so be it. Japan had done this with great success, and they followed the same process.

Table 1 reveals the impact of such policies followed by Asian countries, which accumulated dollars mainly in the form of bonds issued by the US federal government. In March 1986, the foreign ownership of US bonds equaled $273 billion. Ten years later, the value had jumped to $1,199 billion. To be sure, some non-Asian countries, especially Britain, Canada and Germany, also accumulated more US bonds, but the bulk of the new bonds were bought by Asians.

Table 1: Foreign Ownership of US Government Bonds

Years	Foreign Ownership of Bonds (billions of dollars)
March 1987	273
1988	333
1989	377
1990	422
1991	464
1992	508
1993	564
1994	633
1995	729
1996	932
March 1997	1199

Source: Office of the Under Secretary for Domestic
Finance, The Bureau of the Public Debt, May 1997.

In the seven years between 1987 and 1994, foreign

ownership climbed from $273 billion to $633 billion or by $360 billion. But in the next three years, foreign-holdings rose much faster — from 633 to 1,199 or by $566 billion. In other words, the pace of foreign ownership of US bonds has accelerated since 1993. In 1996 alone, foreign holdings soared by $260 billion.

There are two reasons for this. First, the US trade deficit or the rest of the world's trade surplus continues to rise. Second, because of extremely low interest rates, a lot of Japanese money has moved into US bonds which pay much more.

Japan's continued interest in American assets is rather puzzling, because many Japanese companies lost huge amounts of money from their US investments in the 1980s. They had invested big in US real estate and factories, but the continued fall in American inflation and currency simply crippled the value of such investments. Since 1991, however, when Japan moved into a recession, Japanese money has gone mostly into American bonds, although some has moved into American stocks as well. Japan's hefty purchases are mainly responsible for the over $200 billion jump in foreign holdings of US bonds in each of 1995 and 1996.

For 1997, the trade deficit was at an all-time high of over $200 billion; it is bound to set another record in foreign acquisition of American bonds.

The Center and the Peripheries

How do we explain the world's extreme interest in American assets? As mentioned earlier, in the 1970s other nations were not ready to hold American dollars indefinitely. They wanted gold instead for their export surplus. But not anymore. It is hard to explain this phenomenon without comparing it with similar events in colonial empires.

In every empire, there is a center that is surrounded by other states. The center is under the direct control of the ruling people and elites, while the states are under their indirect control. Representatives of the ruling elites run the colonies to further the interests of the imperial nation. They collect gifts and taxes and pass them onto the center. Their own power and privileges are tied to the well-being of the rulers. Provincial elites work to keep the central elites in power to perpetuate their own hold on their people. Thus the self interest of territorial governors appointed by Rome was linked to the interest of the Roman generals. The two acted in unison to enrich themselves and remain in power.

In today's business empire, America is at the center, while most other countries represent the surrounding states. The governors of these states are not appointed by America, but they see their self-interest tied with the interest of the American elites. Japan wants a prosperous America so it can keep its export machine alive and prevent a rise in its unemployment. Thus the Bank of Japan continues to buy American bonds, keeping American interest rates low and the economy strong; China and some other countries do the same.

As foreign individuals and central banks purchase US bonds, they end up investing billions of dollars in the American economy every year. This is the secret of the US prosperity in the 1980s and the 1990s. However, almost all the foreign money goes into consumption for which the bill would come due someday, perhaps in the near future. As we shall see in Chapter 3, there are two types of trade deficits-- consumption driven and investment driven. Of the two, only the investment driven trade shortfall brings lasting prosperity. The other kind may destroy the economy in the end.

The interests of the rich in America are linked to those of the rich in other nations. The effect of all these voluntary arrangements is that goods and services from the rest of the world flow at no cost into the center, which is the United

States. This is how the American business empire thrives. In theory this process could last forever; at least that is what the US elites hope and preach to the people. But it is clearly an artificial arrangement, and cannot go on and on, with the world exchanging its surplus goods for paper money.

* * *

2. Asian Tigers: Real or Paper

The Asian stock market crashes of 1997 began with a currency crisis in the month of July in Thailand and quickly spread to nations next door. One by one, overheated markets crashed in Hong Kong, Singapore, Taiwan and South Korea, all of which, because of their rapid industrialization, have been called "little tigers." Subsequently, four others were added to the original list: Indonesia, Malaysia, Thailand and the Philippines, which are also called "baby tigers," or the cubs of Asia. The combined list of these eight countries may be called the Asian tigers. Thus, the list includes four little tigers and four cubs or baby tigers.

Incidentally, China, because of its giant size, is not included in the list, although the country has had the world's fastest growth in the 1980s and 1990s. It is worth noting that in spite of phenomenal growth rates of the tigers, Japan, because of a large population and an earlier start, is still the dominant economy of Asia.

Since all of them suffered heavy stock price losses in 1997, some experts have questioned the underlying strength of the tigers. Others have called them unstable and corrupt. Lumping them together is unfair, because some of them like Singapore and Hong Kong have little corruption.

Common Features

In spite of their linguistic and cultural differences, the Asian tigers have some common features that led to rapid economic development. Korea is the largest of the tigers. In fact, one Korean economy equals the size of the four baby cubs. Two of the eight tigers, Hong Kong and Singapore, have adopted free trade, while others have been protectionist to varying degrees. But most of them have had high rates of saving and have adopted export-oriented growth strategies. Some have been more prone to exporting then others, but almost all of them have trade surpluses with the United States.

Some people confuse an export-focused economic strategy with free trade. The two may, in fact, be very different. Free trade means low or zero taxes (also known as tariffs) on imports. In other words, free trade is an import-oriented policy, which may or may not be combined with export-led development. Actually, most of the tigers have export driven economies rather than free trade. The strategy has produced exceptional growth rates, as high as 10% per year.

Little Tigers

The growth experience of the four tigers is divided into two periods--one from 1965 to 1980 and the other from 1980 to 1997. In both periods, GDP growth rates, ranging from 6-10%, were extremely high, especially when you realize that average annual growth in the advanced economies of G-7 countries (Canada, Britain, Italy, Germany, Japan, France, and

44

the United States) between 1985 and 1997 was less than 4%. Except in Singapore, both exports and imports grew faster

Table 2. Trade Growth in Little Tigers, (average annual rate in %): 1965-1997

	Export Growth		Import Growth	
	1965-80	1980-97	1965-80	1980-97
Hong Kong	9.1	15.4	8.3	12.6
Korea	27.2	11.6	15.2	10.0
Singapore	4.7	13.5	7.0	9.7
Taiwan	15.6	13.0	12.2	10.0

Source: *World Development Report*(The World Bank), 1991 and *World Economic Outlook* (IMF), 1997

than GDP in the other three countries during both periods. Furthermore, in the other three, export growth outpaced the expansion of imports. (see Table 2) All this shows that their economies were driven by exports.

Singapore is an exception in the first period, when a hefty annual growth of 10% was accompanied only by a 4.7% growth in exports and a 7% growth in imports. Thus, trade was the lagging sector in Singapore in its early stage of development. However, in the second period, Singapore's export and import growth rates exceeded its GDP expansion, and the country joined the other tigers in the export orientation of development.

Korea and Taiwan stand out in this group, Korea for a sharp decline and Taiwan for a sharp rise in growth of exports over time. It may be noted that GDP growth fell for every nation in

45

the second period, even though it was still impressive when compared to the performance of other countries; this was a sign of maturity in the tiger economies.

Baby Tigers

The development experience of the four baby tigers is displayed in Table 3 for the same period as 1965 to 1997. The babies have clearly not grown as fast as the little tigers, but, except for the Philippines, they enjoyed respectable growth, especially relative to the rest of the world.

Table 3. Trade Growth in Baby Tigers (average annual percentages): 1965-1997

	Export Growth		Import Growth	
	1965-80	1980-97	1965-80	1980-97
Indonesia	9.6	5.6	NA	4
Malaysia	4.6	12	2.2	9.1
Philippines	4.6	5.1	2.9	6.6
Thailand	8.6	14.0	4.1	12.2

Source: Same as Table 2.

Another distinguishing feature of this group is that exports were not an extraordinary factor in its performance.

In the first period, Malaysia and the Philippines saw exports lag behind output expansion, whereas the other two saw exports outpace output but not by much. So during the second period, Malaysia and Thailand reveal a clear-cut export orientation in their economy with double-digit export growth rates, but Indonesia and the Philippines pull back in this respect. The Philippines, in fact, suffered a huge shortfall in the rate of development, which was clearly not worthy of a tiger.

Another crucial difference between little and baby tigers is in the level of external debt. Among the little tigers, only Korea has large debt amounting to $110 billion, but relative to its economy, the debt is small; the other three have huge reserves of foreign exchange.

However, each of the baby tigers is a large debtor to the world. In fact, the main source of their growth in recent years seems to be their foreign borrowing, which takes the shine away from their growth performance. Every nation in this group, except Thailand, saw a fall in annual growth in the second period, even though debt grew much faster than output. Thailand did improve upon its rate of development, but mainly with the help of foreign loans.

All this can be clearly seen in Table 4. Indonesia is among the world's largest debtor nations, with an external debt of $108 billion in 1995. Others don't owe so much to the world, but their accumulated borrowing is still a large percentage of their GDP. Thus, the growth performance of the baby tigers, though impressive on the whole, is sullied by their mountains of external debt, which has the seeds of instability. This is what happened in Thailand, which was forced to curtail its development plans, and that has caused unexpected pain in terms of job losses and wage cuts. By the end of 1997, Thai foreign debt had ballooned to $97 billion.

Indonesia's debt at 57% of GDP is also worrisome; others have similar troubles as well. The conclusion is clear: The tiger economies, except for Indonesia and the Philippines, have followed an export-oriented strategy for development since the

Table 4. External Debt (billions of dollars)

	Debt Level		Debt as % of GDP	
	1980	1995	1980	1995
Indonesia	21	108	28	57
Malaysia	7	34	28	43
Philippines	17	39	54	52
Thailand	8	57	26	35

Source: Same as in Table 2

mid-1960s. They have succeeded admirably in raising the general standard of living and performed much better than those developing economies--such as India, Brazil and Mexico--that relied on regional monopolies at home to create a high growth environment.

It so happens that India and Latin America adopted import-oriented policies to replace imports with domestic production. They followed the history of the United States, Canada and Australia, which became advanced economies in the 19th century under the umbrella of tariffs and import-substituting measures. However, they forgot that the advanced western economies had not only adopted high tariffs, but had also encouraged stiff competition among domestic industries, which needed little foreign rivalry, as they faced vigorous competition with local firms.

The astounding economic success of the tigers does not show that protectionism is bad, but that protectionism combined with domestic monopolies is bad. Japan did extremely well with protectionism and turned its economy from total devastation during the Second World War into an industrial giant in just 40 years. The secret of its success was import substitution in an environment of cutthroat domestic competition.

In the end, it is competition that really counts. A country with a large population does not need export markets to enjoy the efficient production that comes with large-scale factories. That is why Japan, India and Brazil don't need foreign markets but they do need domestic competition.

However, countries with smaller populations, which most of the tigers are, need export markets, and for them an export-oriented strategy is desirable. After all, America, with tariffs on manufacturing as high as 100%, became the world industrial leader in the 19th century in a matter of 60 years. In the process, the highly protected country beat out the economies of Britain, France, Italy and Germany, which had had a head start and a long lead in the race for industrial revolution.

The South East Asian Miracle

Is it just coincidence that among a dozen or so rapidly growing economies of the world between 1965 and 1997, eight were located in a single region called South East Asia? The eight include China, the four tigers and the three Asian cubs (Malaysia, Indonesia and Thailand). Even excluding Japan, Asia has been the fastest growing region since the mid-1960s. Of course, with Japan included, Asia easily wins the growth race. We will study Japan separately in the next chapter, because by the mid-1970s Japan had joined the elite group of

49

developed nations, while others, though prospering apace, were still not in the same league.

We have already examined one secret of East Asia's phenomenal success, namely the export-orientation of the little tigers and cubs. But we have also seen that historically import-oriented development was just as successful as the export-oriented strategy. So there must be some other factors behind the South East Asian economic miracle. These have been studied extensively by scholars before.

The four Asian tigers, like Japan, have few natural resources but a high population density. This makes their legendary success all the more remarkable. What the tigers did have was an educated and disciplined labor force ready to develop new skills. After 1960, all four nations spent heavily on higher education and built new learning facilities. They sent their brightest students abroad, especially the United States, to study new technology. Initially, a crucial factor in Korea and Taiwan was the US aid and export of technology, although this was not much of a factor in the city states of Hong Kong and Singapore.

During 25 years of development since 1950, Korea received the equivalent of $500 per person in aid from the United States, whereas Taiwan received $425 per capita. But some other countries such as India and Pakistan that also obtained large amounts of foreign assistance did not show as much promise as the two tigers. Foreign investment, aid and technology were important in the development of Korea and Taiwan, but once the growth engine had been started, its speed was maintained by local saving, technology and investment.

Unlike Korea and Taiwan, Hong Kong received little aid from abroad even in its early stage of development. Even private foreign investment was not forthcoming, as much of that investment at that time used to go into the production of raw materials which the city-state lacked. Consequently, Hong Kong, a British colony at the time, launched a program of labor-intensive industrialization, concentrating on light industries like textiles, electric items and wristwatches.

Much of this production went to Britain and the United States, both of which were busy opening their markets. In fact, Western trade liberalization helped all the little tigers and subsequently the cubs. But Hong Kong was the first to take the export initiative, and today it is perhaps the richest city in Asia, even richer than Japan in terms of after-tax per capita income.

Singapore, by contrast, followed a totally different route. Like Korea and Taiwan, Singapore sparked its development engine with the help of foreign assistance, but the assistance came from private sources in the form of direct foreign investment rather than government aid. Multinational corporations from Europe and the United States were attracted to the area because of its cheap, disciplined and educated labor force and because of its lower taxes.

In the early stage of development, the four tigers focused on light manufacturing that needed little capital but required skilled labor. In other words, early industrialization concentrated on labor-intensive manufacturing.

Once surplus labor was absorbed by light industries, the tigers went after high-tech enterprises needing more capital per person. This way productivity rose even faster than before and it also made wage gains possible for workers. The fruit of industrialization then spread among the general population. That is why the tiger economies have lower income disparities than many advanced and developing economies.

Low disparity is another factor that helped launch and

sustain a long process of industrialization and development. This is because low-income disparity is normally associated with low political and bureaucratic corruption. Corrupt bureaucracies have hindered development in many nations, but this was not a problem in tiger economies. In fact, tiger bureaucracies understood the need for attracting foreign capital, developing infrastructure for smooth transportation and communication, and focusing on technical education to generate skilled labor.

Low-income inequality resulted from government policy and economic legislation that included land reforms in Korea and Taiwan and the provision of inexpensive public housing in Hong Kong and Singapore. The purpose of reforms in all cases was to make the basic necessities affordable to everyone.

Finally, the governments encouraged thrift either through laws that kept taxes low on interest income, or through fiscal discipline that restrained budget deficits and inflation. At a time when much of the world adopted deficit budgets in times of high or low unemployment, the tigers kept government spending under control. This way they avoided persistent inflation and encouraged savings, as people were not afraid that rising prices could erode the value of their money. In fact, after the early stage of development, the tigers, with their restrained inflation, enjoyed persistent export surpluses, which enabled them to avoid foreign debt and the resulting crisis that engulfed some developing economies in the 1980s.

It may be noted that direct foreign investment does not create debt problems for a country; the problem arises when a government or a country's private companies borrow money from abroad. This is how the legendary debt problems of Mexico, Brazil, Indonesia and now Korea were born.

Fiscal discipline is one of the noted achievements of Asian

tigers, because the rest of the world, including the G-7 countries, had large and persistent budget deficits. Even now budget shortfalls plague both Western and Eastern Europe, Japan and many other countries. But the tigers have, by and large, kept their fiscal house in order by adopting low deficit policies.

Swimming against the flow is never easy. As with the rest of the world, Korea suffered from high inflation in the late 1970s. But through a policy of wage and spending restraint, the government quickly restored an environment of stable inflation.

High savings eventually result in high investment. The fiscal discipline of the tigers led to exceptionally large rates of investment. As late as 1990, Korea committed 37% of its GDP to investment. Singapore did the same. So did Hong Kong and Taiwan to some extent. Compared to the US investment rate of 15%, the tigers' rate was and is phenomenal. Not surprisingly, their productivity also grew sharply after 1960, and has continued to this day.

Asian Cubs

Compared to the four tigers, the four cubs of Asia have not been as successful, but compared to the rest of the world, their achievements are, on the whole, impressive. As shown before, except for the Philippines, Indonesia, Malaysia and Thailand have substantially raised the living standard of their people.

The cubs have followed a somewhat different track. The first generation of tigers had few natural resources, but the second generation was well endowed with them. However, the babies failed to grow fast until they began exporting manufactured goods. The cubs were latecomers to the club of rapid development. But they adopted some of the measures so successful in their neighbors and became fast movers in the process.

One common feature of their success is the large investment that they attracted from Japan and the little tigers. They too had a disciplined and educated labor force. They too had fiscal discipline and stability. All this combined with low wage costs made them very attractive to Japanese firms that were overly burdened by an expensive currency. Currency appreciation makes exports dearer but imports cheaper. The yen had been appreciating ever since 1972 relative to the dollar; it stabilized in the early 1980s, but resumed its rise after 1985.

Attracted by cheap currencies and labor, Japanese corporations opened factories in the cub economies, especially Thailand and Malaysia. Production from these factories went partly back to Japan but mostly to the United States. This way the relatively weak cub economies managed to penetrate US markets. They suffered trade deficits with Japan, but developed trade surpluses with America in the 1980s and the 1990s. After accessing the American markets, Malaysia and Thailand became one of the fastest growing countries in the world.

Later Taiwan and Korea also offered aid to the baby tigers. However, the Philippines failed to follow the tracks of its neighbors even though foreign investment and technology was as accessible to this country as to others. This shows that foreign aid and investment alone are not enough for sustained and rapid development. Domestic conditions must also be favorable.

Unlike the little tigers, the Philippines failed to develop a competitive environment at home by breaking up regional monopolies. The lack of domestic competition meant shoddy products and high and noncompetitive prices. Moreover, the country also suffered from high income and wealth disparities that created an atmosphere of corruption and bureaucratic inefficiency.

Indonesia suffers from the same internal problems as the Philippines. How did it then manage a stronger pace of development? There is a crucial difference between the two countries. Indonesia's oil wealth enabled it to surge ahead during the 1970s when oil prices soared around the world. But the development pace slowed sharply in the early 1980s, when the oil price began to tumble. At that point, the country tried state intervention by directing its savings into heavy and capital-intensive industries. Its regional monopolies prospered behind walls of import tariffs, but development suffered.

Between 1985 and 1988, Indonesia made an about-turn. It cut tariffs, encouraged foreign investment, reduced state penetration of industry, and also slightly expanded domestic competition. Such economic reforms stimulated the pace of development, and expanded non-oil exports. Still the country remains one of the largest debtors in the world, thanks to all the government waste that occurred in the 1980s.

Economic Diversity

So far we have emphasized the common features underlying the tiger economies. We have seen that most of them have adopted an export-driven path of development along with a hefty contribution from foreign investment and fiscal discipline; they all relied on tax policies that promoted saving and investment, and so on. However, they have important differences as well.

The main difference lies in the role of the state in various countries. Hong Kong is the only nation that steered clear of an active regulation of industries. There the government intervened little in the behavior of labor, product, financial and stock markets, except in times of crises such as the one that occurred in 1983, when the Hong Kong dollar was pegged to the US dollar at a rate of 7.8 to 1. The peg has worked well so far and still remains in effect.

Hong Kong is a model of private enterprise in most sectors except land and property. All land is owned by the government and leased to the people. The state thus holds a monopoly over undeveloped land, much of which was created through reclamation from the sea. Land is released for public use in accordance with a plan that is publicized a year in advance. Then some areas are leased to the highest bidder in a public auction. The leaseholder is required to develop the released area for a certain purpose such as housing, shopping malls and office buildings.

During the Second World War, much of the stock of housing was destroyed in Hong Kong. With the huge inflow of refugees from china, an acute housing shortage developed in the territory. Consequently, the government imposed rent controls on all pre-war housing. In 1970, the controls were extended on houses constructed after the war as well. These measures have been renewed ever since, although the government intends to rescind them some day.

The state intervention in the property sector also takes the form of public housing, which the government builds to provide affordable shelter. Nearly half the people live in public apartments. Another 20% live in rent controlled residences. In spite of heavy state intervention, the property market is very active and profitable in Hong Kong. There has been great speculation in this sector. Residential real estate prices have far outpaced the rate of inflation.

There are two main reasons for this. One lies in negative real rate of interest, which equals the rate that people actually pay on loans minus the rate of inflation. The idea behind this concept is simple. Interest earned adds to the value of a person's money; inflation, on the other hand, destroys the value of money; therefore, net return from money lending is the interest rate less the rate of inflation. This is the real rate. If inflation exceeds the interest rate, a person essentially borrows money at a negative rate. This gives speculators great incentive to buy property with borrowed funds and then sell it at inflated prices.

The other reason for property inflation is a strong monetary boom, because someone has to pay money to buy things at higher prices. The Hong Kong dollar has been linked to foreign currencies for much of its post-war history, either the British pound or the US dollar. As a result the island's money supply is linked to its trade balance, which has been in a perennial surplus.

Export surplus brings foreign money and an import surplus causes a loss of foreign exchange. In a pegged exchange system, the foreign exchange inflow raises money supply at home. For instance, since 1983, for each US dollar in reserve, Hong Kong authorities are entitled to issue 7.8 Hong Kong dollars. This means that money supply rises in direct proportion to the trade surplus or the inflow of foreign exchange.

When you combine high money growth with negative real interest rates, you have the makings of a speculative mania leading to soaring asset prices. One asset that climbed repeatedly in value was property; the other was the stock price of various companies. Therefore, the reasons behind the property and share price booms are essentially the same. Of course, property companies, because of their robust profit growth, saw the fastest rise in share values. Hence, it is interesting that the government allowed the market forces a free hand in most sectors, but extensively intervened in the real estate industry. This may have been partly responsible for extreme speculation in the economy.

Other tiger economies have adopted industrial policies with varying degrees of success and failure. The term industrial policy means that the state actively allocates national resources and foreign exchange toward priority industries. A planning body determines what industrial priorities are. In this respect, Singapore stands on top. It had the heaviest state intervention among all the tigers. The government even owned and operated some factories, but the governing principles were those followed by private corporations.

The private sector aims at minimizing production cost and maximizing quality in order to earn the highest profit. The production ministries in Singapore did the same in order to export their goods in world markets. The government also intervened in labor markets by setting wages; initially, wages were kept low to attract multinational corporations, but were raised sharply in the 1970s to induce the companies to adopt capital-using and labor-saving technologies. Thus, labor productivity rose in tandem with rising wages, and the country remained competitive in global markets. It still has a positive balance of trade.

Korea also actively pursued an industrial policy, initially relying on labor-intensive, but export-oriented industries. The country also adopted protectionist policies to stimulate capital-intensive manufacturing that faced tough competition from Japan and Western economies. In the early 1970s, the government turned to heavy and chemical industry (HCI) to build six industries through increased tariffs and subsidized credit.

Banks were told to lend money to certain sectors; wages were controlled as in Singapore. The idea was that the six industries including steel, chemicals, ship building and electronics among others would become world-class competitors and promote exports. The program was a success in some respects and a failure in others.

The nation's export drive was indeed successful; but the tight control on the financial system led to some weak banks that had to be bailed out. Even today the banking system operates under some controls. Eventually, the government abandoned the HCI program, liberalized trade and loosened its grip on banking. In recent years, the wage policy has also been abandoned, and worker earnings have risen dramatically.

From the mid-1990s, increasing trade liberalization has resulted in growing trade deficits, which create big problems because Korea has a large foreign debt. As long as trade is in surplus, the debt can be easily managed. Otherwise, it can create a major currency and economic crisis.

The government also played a solid role in Taiwan. Its focus initially was on land reform to expand farm output and free the country from dependence on food imports. In the early 1950s, the state adopted protectionist policies, but then turned to export promotion after 1958. It also extended an invitation to multinational corporations, frequently offering them tax concessions. Protectionism made a return in the 1970s, but was slowly abandoned in the early 1980s. Ever since then the economy has generated a huge export surplus and vast foreign exchange reserves, which the country has used partly for foreign aid.

It must be clear by now that except for Hong Kong, the state played a crucial role in the economic development of the little tigers. But the role differed from country to country. Today, the state intervention has declined, but the various governments continue to keep an active watch over economic and especially export performance. Let us now see what the state did in the economies of the baby tigers.

As mentioned earlier, the baby tigers, unlike the first generation, were vastly endowed with natural resources. As a result, the state intervention followed a different track in the cub economies. Initially, the governments adopted a policy of minimum intervention. Take for instance, the case of Malaysia. Because of its natural wealth, many multinational companies were attracted to the area. Foreign investment and high local savings enabled the country to grow at high rates for a long time.

Malaysia did adopt planning but mostly for rural development. In the first three five-year plans (1956-1970), the state essentially had no industrial policy. But the economic course changed dramatically after 1970. From 1971 to 1985, the state intervened heavily to launch a program of rapid industrialization and to lower income and wealth disparity that had arisen from market-led development.

At the start of 1981, the government tilted full scale toward protectionism and import substitution. It followed the Korean model; in fact, it invited Korean experts to design a program of industrialization with a focus on heavy industry. However, unlike in Korea, the program failed miserably in Malaysia. Most of the public enterprises lost money; the government then adopted a strategy of privatization to expand domestic competition, which had so far been lacking. Privatization has been a great success, helping to sustain the country's long period of development.

The state's role in Indonesia has been more or less similar to that in Korea and Malaysia. The Indonesian government adopted import-substitution at one time and then switched to export promotion. However, Indonesia went much further and in the process built up a bigger pile of debt than both Korea and Malaysia. Korea's state-dominated approach to development has not been successful in the economies of baby tigers.

Because of its natural resources and a close link with the United States, the Philippines was in the best position among its neighbors to have an economic surge. Yet, it has had the worst record of all the tigers. Many experts blame the government and poor leadership for its poor economic performance. Others put the blame on the political instability of the Marcos regime in the 1980s. The economy has improved somewhat since 1994, but the country still has a long way to go.

Finally, let us examine the role of the state in Thailand, which has been another Asian nation with stellar growth over a long period of time. The country got off to a poor start as state monopolies combined with protectionism actually caused a decline in Thai GDP per person in the early 1950s. Then the government changed course, shifted its focus to private enterprise and exports. Since 1955 the economy has been growing robustly and steadily, while tariffs stayed at high levels until 1980.

It is interesting that the extraordinary level of Thai growth occurred against the backdrop of a low rate of investment. From 1955 to 1988, the investment share of GDP averaged 25%, somewhat below the levels in Korea and Singapore.

Yet the steady growth rate of over 7% was quite impressive. In the 1990s, investment, both domestic and foreign, has soared, and the growth has risen a little. In 1995, for instance, the investment share of GDP was a lofty 43%.

Overall, Thai economic intervention has been neither as meager as in Hong Kong nor as pervasive as in Korea and Singapore. Actually, the Thai government did seek to have a strong influence on the course of development by focusing on heavy, capital-intensive industries. But political and bureaucratic corruption, resulting from rising inequality, thwarted many state policies.

Environmental Pollution

The Asian miracle has come at a phenomenal cost to the environment. All tigers suffer from air and water pollution. Taipei, Taiwan has one of the worst air qualities in the world, not only because the city is surrounded by hills, but also because there are six million cars on the tiny island. Indonesia suffers from the same pollution turmoil that afflicts other tigers.

A major source of foul air there is the burning of forests. In fact, in the summer of 1997, forest fires created a cloud of smoke that stretched across all of South East Asia. It covered the whole region for days with a blanket of haze that made breathing difficult.

Traffic jams are common in big cities. Bangkok, Thailand has some of the worst air in the world. Not only does stalled traffic damage the quality of life, but it also adds to air pollution from cars, trucks, buses and scooters that frequently clog the roads. One little accident, and the traffic comes to a halt for hours.

Heavy industrialization has also contaminated rivers and lakes. In Malaysia, Indonesia and Korea, petrochemicals are the big culprits. In Hong Kong and Singapore, water pollution springs mainly from the heavy population density. There are simply too many people residing on tiny islands. The environmental problems could prove a drag on growth in the future.

Recent Developments

Pushed by the United States, the tigers have had to liberalize trade not only in manufacturing but also in services. Until the 1980s, except for Hong Kong and Singapore, the tigers maintained high tariff or non-tariff barriers against the imports of capital-intensive, high-tech industries. They also restricted foreign access to banking, insurance and stock markets.

However, in the 1990s the tariff rates have been gradually lowered and foreign investments permitted in financial sectors. Capital has become far more mobile internationally than ever before. As a result of trade liberalization and the inflow of foreign capital, imports have been soaring in some tiger economies such as Korea, Malaysia and Thailand with a serious deterioration in their balance of trade.

A negative trade balance normally hurts growth; but the tigers have seen a marked increase in foreign investment in their factories as well as stock markets. This has neutralized the negative consequences of rising trade deficits, and growth has remained strong.

With large inflows of foreign money also came high speculation in real estate and stock markets. Most people would count it as another positive factor, but speculative bubbles create an element of instability. When the bubble

63

bursts, there is a lot of pain from industrial retrenchment and from recessions that normally follow. With their economies growing rapidly for such a long period, a recession is unthinkable in the politics of the Asian tigers. But speculative manias can kill the best of economies. Is the unthinkable possible? We shall see in subsequent chapters.

It should be clear by now that the experts who have ridiculed East Asian economies as paper tigers are totally wrong. The tigers have made tremendous progress in many different sectors and eradicated poverty for the vast majority of their people; some have done this without even the gift of natural resources.

The tigers are for real; but they could be reduced to the flimsiness of paper in the near future, thanks to all the financial deregulation that American experts and policy makers have forced upon them. We will examine this premise in detail in the pages that follow.

* * *

3. Japan: The Ailing Lion

The role model that the Asian tigers followed diligently was the one prospering right in their backyard, namely Japan. They watched their neighbor with admiration, as the land of the rising sun, devastated by atom bombs in the Second World War, first stood on its feet, swiftly penetrated the markets of the global giant, the United States, and then achieved the status of an economic super power, all in a matter of three to four decades. They saw how a protectionist Japan, endowed with few natural resources except an educated and workaholic labor force, built an industrial machine and then turned it into an export locomotive, first relying on low-tech, labor-intensive goods and then excelling in high-tech, capital-intensive industries.

Japan had started with a planned economy, and then gradually liberalized a few of its institutions, mostly under pressure from US experts. It tightly controlled credit that was directed to sectors considered important for industrialization. Japan's message impressed its pupils in the neighborhood, as they adopted the track of industrial policy and not western style free enterprise, at least at the outset of growth.

The first generation of Asian tigers faced the same dilemma as Japan: how do you transform a war-ravaged economy into an island of peace and prosperity? For their territorial security, some of them aligned themselves with the United States, as did Japan. Korea and Taiwan were directly under the umbrella of US protection, whereas Hong Kong was a British colony and indirectly linked with NATO and the US allies. This way the defense burden could be lightened, and the countries could focus on the crucial task of survival.

Since 1990, Japan has suffered either from recession or stagnation. Its real estate and stock markets are in turmoil, and banks and insurance companies are in trouble. All this has indeed taken the gloss off the Japanese miracle, but Japan still remains the second largest economy in the world. Moreover, the United States is Japan's biggest borrowing client, having accepted close to a trillion dollars in loans since 1983. If its neighbors are the tigers, Japan is the lion of Asia, albeit an ailing lion now.

In order to understand where the world stands today, we have to fully analyze the history of the Japanese miracle, and why that miracle has faded in the 1990s. I believe there has been a Japanization of East Asia and Latin America in this decade, and Japan's economic flu, while already infecting the neighborhood, will soon spread around the world. After all, Japan is the second largest economy on earth, and any earthquake there cannot but have global reverberations.

Japanization of Asia

What do I mean by the term "Japanization?" The term signifies a model of export-led development coupled with a stock market bubble inflated by a monetary or credit boom.

Export-led development occurs when a nation industrializes primarily to meet foreign tastes and demand, and only secondarily to improve home wages and consumption.

At the early stage of development, this is perhaps the only way to achieve a rapid economic rise. In 1950, Japan needed raw materials and foreign technology. It made perfect sense for Japan to concentrate on exports at that time. However, the country did not need an export surplus; balanced trade would have produced the same results, and perhaps better. The trouble is that in Japan and among its followers, the export focus turned into an export obsession. As you will see, this, combined with America's obsession with globalization and financial deregulation, has now brought the world economy to the brink of collapse.

An export obsessed economy needs foreign markets to grow; having neglected the demand side of the economy at home, it is at the mercy of foreign countries and their economic policies. Its trade surplus rises with foreign growth, because there is little demand growth at home. This way an export-obsessed economy becomes an eyesore in the world, which must then suffer a trade deficit. This is what Japan became in the 1980s and even more so in the 1990s.

Another feature of a Japanized economy is a stock market bubble caused by booming growth in credit and money. It is not that Japan, as in the 1970s and the 1980s, was the first to experience a share-price mania; the United States had gone through the same process in the 1920s. But Japan's mania scaled new heights and was supported not by a profit but a credit boom. That is what separated the Japanese asset bubble from the US bubble in the 1920s. Both bubbles burst in the end, as they all do, creating unexpected troubles in the process.

At the end of 1997, Japan's banking system was on the

67

verge of collapse. The banks had lent generously to the tigers, which were beginning to slow down. The fear was that further losses would openly bankrupt some large lending houses, which had been kept solvent by some of the lowest interest rates in the history of Japan. From international standards, several banks were already insolvent, but deposit interest rates barely above 1% had kept the cost of funds so low that they had stayed in business.

Earlier in September, the Ministry of Finance reported a sharp decline in GDP, at a quarterly rate of 3% or an annual rate of 12%, which, if continued, meant the nation was already in depression. The future appeared even gloomier. Because of its large foreign debt along with a hefty trade deficit, the neighboring Korea quickly became a victim of the currency crisis that had begun in Thailand in July. The resulting capital flight caused a sharp depreciation of the Korean won. Suddenly, the country woke up to find that its foreign debt woes had multiplied. Indebted banks and corporations needed far more wons to finance the dollars they had borrowed from abroad.

The depreciation of the won meant that the already weakening yen would have to fall further. A depreciated currency can cause a great deal of inflation, as it did in Mexico during the peso crisis in 1995. When countries compete with each other in international markets, losses by one currency quickly spread to neighboring countries. This is the dictate of markets. But Japan already had a vast trade surplus with the rest of the world, which was sure to resist further cheapening of Japanese goods abroad.

If the yen fell as much in value as the won, Korea and Japan would see no change in the prices of their goods in each other's markets. But both would see a fall in their product prices in other nations, because a cheap currency means cheaper goods priced in that currency.

With the world already flooded with Japan's goods, this was likely to create tensions, especially in Europe and the United States. However, if Japan could not match the won's devaluation, it was sure to lose a lot of business to Korean companies. That is why an already weakened Japan stood at the brink of a steep recession and even a depression at the end of 1997.

Why did it have to come this? Why did the country not cure its economy, wasting seven precious years after 1990, when its troubles first began? To comprehend this we have to study the course of economic development followed by Japan. We have to examine how the country's politics and bureaucracy work.

Era Of Rapid Growth

Post-war Japan is an amazing story of recovery, reconstruction and world economic leadership in many areas. The country rose literally from the ashes and developed into a giant in just a quarter of a century after 1950. When a nation grows at a rate of 3% to 4% per year, American economists consider it a great achievement. But from 1950 to 1973 the compound growth rate in Japan was over 10%. Such fast growth for such a long period has not been duplicated by any other country in recorded history. In the process, Japan was totally transformed. The stigma and shame of defeat in the war disappeared. Instead, the nation became a model for other aspiring countries.

Growth during the 1950s was slightly below 10% per year, while in the 1960s, it was slightly above that figure. But in both decades, the vast majority of the population

69

experienced a great jump in prosperity. Labor productivity rose sharply, and so did the average real wage. Table 5 presents data for the real wage index, national tax burden, after-tax wage and per-capita real GDP, using 1990 as the base year. The national tax burden is the percentage of national taxes, local taxes and social insurance fees to national income.

Table 5 shows that per-capita GDP, after adjustment for inflation, rose from a mere 0.38 million yen in 1950 to as much as 2.04 million yen in 1973. This is a jump of 437% in just 23 years. The real wage index before taxes went up from 19.5 in 1950 to 79.4 in 1973, a jump of 307% over the same period. Since 307 divided by 437 equals 0.703, the rise in real wage was 70.3% of the rise in national productivity.

Even in terms of after-tax wages, the Japanese living standard soared. The national tax burden rose between 1955 and 1975, but mainly because of rising social security expenditures. The percentage of national and local taxes was more or less constant. The after-tax real wage index rose from 21 in 1955 to 59.5 in 1973--a jump of 182%. However, the real wage rise during this period of rapid growth was not smooth. You can see this in Table 6, which transforms the data of Table 5 into growth rates.

From 1950 to 1955, the wage growth more or less matched the growth in productivity. But in the next ten years, wage growth was about half of the productivity rise. In the following eight years, however, wages caught up with productivity, as wage growth nearly equalled the growth in productivity. This suggests that real wages initially lagged behind the rise in labor efficiency; it is perhaps a reflection of the ups and downs in the strength of trade unions. When trade unions are strong, wages rise faster, and when they are weak, wage growth is slow and even negative.

70

Table 5. Real Wage Indexes of Regular Employees, and Real Per Capita GDP, 1950-1975, (1990 = 100)

Year	Real Wage	National Tax Burden(%)	After-Tax Wage	Per- Capita GDP
1950	19.5	NA	NA	0.38
1955	26.4	20	21.1	0.52
1960	33.1	20	26.5	0.77
1965	39.8	22.7	30.8	1.12
1970	58.6	24.3	44.4	1.77
1973	79.4	25.0	59.5	2.04
1975	80.2	25.8	59.5	2.07

Table 6. Real Wage and Average Productivity Growth: 1955-1975 (in percent)

Year	Wage Growth	After-Tax Wage Growth	Productivity Growth
1955	35.4	--	36.8
1960	25.4	25.6	48.1
1965	20.2	16.2	45.5
1970	47.2	44.2	58.0
1973	35.5	34.0	15.3
1975	1	0	0

Source: *Japan Statistical Yearbook, 1995; Economic Statistics Annual, 1994; Japan Almanac, 1995; The Postwar Japanese Economy, Second Edition 1995, by Takafusa Nakamura, and The Economic Development of Japan, Second Edition 1994, by Ryoshin Minami.*

The rise in national productivity reflected the efficiency rise in many areas, including agriculture, manufacturing, construction and services. This was a case of balanced growth in which all key industries prospered.

The biggest productivity jump occurred in manufacturing, followed by construction, agriculture and then services. This shows that by nature the highest efficiency growth occurs in the secondary sector, or manufacturing, followed by the primary and the tertiary industries. That is why economic policy should aim at protecting the secondary industries from foreign competition. They add greatly to the living standard.

How did Japan achieve spectacular growth in industrial efficiency, despite a very low starting base? Through the import of capital and technology, and through the peace-time use of own technology developed during the war. The development of war-time technology created the educational and technical base that was peacefully harnessed in Japan after the war. This base was necessary to absorb foreign technology as well, because without educated and skilled workers, new inventions cannot be utilized.

In order to develop a bulwark against communism, the United States encouraged its companies to export technology to Japan. In industry after industry new plant and equipment were imported by Japan. This, of course, created a headache from a negative balance of trade. Steel, ship-building, chemicals, machinery, textiles, electrical power, among many others, were thus transformed by the latest techniques of production. In some industries, Japan's technology was so modern that it was even better than that of their American competitors.

Slowly, but surely, the country marched ahead and became the world leader in the areas of ship-building, textiles, and petrochemicals. But the biggest prize goes to the auto industry, which today is supreme in the world market. Japan made a slow start in this direction in the early 1950s. Nissan, Isuzu and Hino obtained auto technology from Europe, whereas Toyota and Prince developed on their own.

In the second half of the decade, these companies began to build small cars. They were joined by Honda and Subaru in the early 1960s, and after 1965 Japan evolved into a major exporter of cars. Today the country excels in product variety and quality. Japanese cars of all sizes, luxury and diversity now criss-cross the globe.

Economic development of many countries in Europe and North America shows that industrialization is normally accompanied by the mechanization of agriculture, which also then enjoys a rapid rise in productivity. Farm output rises while farm population and labor decline. At the same time, the proportion of labor employed rises in manufacturing, construction and services. The same process occurred in Japan as well, except there it came with exceptional speed.

The proportion of employed labor in the primary industry that includes agriculture, forestry and fisheries fell from 46% in 1951 to just 12.7% in 1975, whereas that of the secondary industry that includes construction and manufacturing rose from 22.5% to 35.2% during the same period. In the tertiary sector, that includes services as well as the transportation and communication industries, the employment proportion jumped from 31% to 52%.

It is clear that after 1950 Japan quickly moved toward a diversified economy, where at least a third of employment occurs in the secondary industry. The nation reached this level by the mid-1960s. The fruit of diversification is strong and it paid a large dividend in terms of the rapidly rising living standard.

The rapid rise in agricultural productivity raised farm income, which had been low before the war. This, along with rising wages in all industries, caused a sharp decline in income inequality. Rising wages and declining inequality in turn meant that consumer spending rose sharply and kept pace with rising production.

Savings as a proportion of national income also soared. This could have caused a great problem of over-production because if the saving rate rises sharply, national demand falls short of national supply, creating excess production in the process. That in turn leads to production cut-backs and unemployment.

In Japan, however, businesses spent large amounts of money on investment and absorbed the country's savings, which rose from a mere 5% rate in 1950 to as high as 25% in 1975. As long as investment spending absorbs savings, demand is large enough to absorb national output, and there is no problem of excess production. In fact, the high rate of saving fostered capital formation, new technology and growth.

Without adequate savings, capital accumulation is not possible. During the 1950s and 1960s, Japan needed capital and the people rose to the occasion. They educated themselves, worked hard and saved large portions of their incomes.

Of course, it is easier to save more when your income rises rapidly, but you also need self-discipline against spending to do the job. While people worked vigorously, such strong growth could not have occurred without proper planning and government policies. What were those policies that generated the economic miracle? This is what we discuss next.

* * *

High Competition

Prior to the war, Japanese industry was highly monopolistic. There were many regional monopolies organised as Zaibatsu. They kept wages low and profits high. They also blocked the entry of other entrepreneurs in their areas and virtually used their workers as serfs. After the defeat, Japan was occupied by the American army. The United States felt that the Zaibatsu had supported Japanese militarism, and so the American government decided to dissolve the monopolies.

The Zaibatsu owners were removed from top positions in their companies and their shares were sold to the public. The occupation authorities also decided to break up other large companies into smaller units. Eighteen such companies, including Nippon Steel, Mitsui Mining, among others, were actually divided into smaller firms. As Economist Takafusa Nakamura concludes: "These measures set the stage for the fierce competition which was characteristic of post-war industry in Japan. As we will see, the plant and equipment expansions and technological advances made under the pressure of competition produced economic growth." (p.27)

High competition in industry was a great gift of the occupation authorities to Japan, which could not have done this on its own. It is very difficult to fight the wealthy interests that control politics, even if their actions are destructive for the nation. The United States government has not been able to introduce the same competition policies in its own country, because such measures are always blocked by business giants and their hired economists.

Once the Obanto (chief managers) of Zaibatsu lost their privileged positions, there arose a trend to hire business executives from the ranks of the younger generation. The young executives were vigorous and visionary. They engaged in fierce competition with each other in terms of product quality and technology. All this stimulated innovation and injected dynamism into the economy. The young managers vied with each other in importing technology and introducing new techniques of management.

In order to keep costs under control, the companies sharply expanded the sub-contracting system that had actually started during the war. In this system, a company assigned the production of different parts to sub-contractors, which were smaller firms and thus paid lower wages.

Prior to the rise of industrial competition, the sub-contractors had been exploited by the giant firms. Now the highly competitive environment made it necessary that new technology should also be passed on to sub-contractors. This way, productivity and wages rose not only in major companies, but also in small sub-contracting firms. Thus, in post-war Japan both large and small corporations flourished.

Protectionism

Protectionism, works well so long as it is combined with domestic competition, as was the case with the United States, Canada and Australia until the 1920s, because it is needed to create efficient and diversified industry that pays high pages. Post-war Japan followed this policy in a variety of ways. The tariff rates were raised on imports of final consumption goods, but most raw materials and capital goods still enjoyed low or no customs duties.

The average tariff on dutiable imports in 1950 jumped from 10% to more than 18%. These tariffs remained high until 1970 when the Kennedy-Round of GATT agreement slowly brought them down.

The allocation of foreign exchange to priority industries was another way to restrain or ban imports. The government drew up a budget for total imports in each quarter and allocated a certain amount of foreign exchange to various industries, mostly to import raw materials. This was an effective way not only to control the direction of industrial development, but also to restrict unwanted imports.

The auto industry was given great priority. No foreign exchange was thus assigned for auto imports, which were effectively banned during the 1950s. This way, the auto industry was assured of the entire domestic market. It could then make risky investments and absorb imported technology, while its high quality was assured by intense domestic competition.

Similarly, the coal industry was protected through import restraints on oil. Import restrictions were high on farm products as well. The government wanted to help farmers by keeping their prices high. That is why high tariffs were imposed on oranges, apples and beef, whereas rice imports were prohibited. This way, the government sought to develop a diversified economy.

During the late 1950s, the US government, under the prodding of big multinational firms, followed the policy of trade liberalization around the world. Japan faced the same pressure as other countries, and it accepted the principle of freer trade. In the 1960s, this pressure intensified and tariff cuts were made by most countries under the Kennedy Round. However, while Japan lowered its tariffs on most industries, it maintained its numerous regulations that effectively restricted imports. This way, Japanese exports grew fast, but imports did not.

Moreover, agriculture remained exempt from the tariff cuts of the Kennedy Round. As a result, farmers continued to keep up with the rising living standard of the rest of the nation. The government went to great lengths to ensure a vibrant farm economy. The Agricultural Land Act of 1952 assured not only price parity to rice farmers, but also income parity. Under the price parity formula the rice price would rise in proportion to prices of industrial goods purchased by farmers. But with income parity, the rice price was greater than that of the price parity formula.

As a consequence of this policy, farm income could rise with that of the rest of the economy. The formula was changed yet again in 1960 to ensure that farm income kept pace with fast rising urban wages.

Traditional economists have sharply denounced the ban of rice imports in Japan. But this was done for a humane purpose, which was to reduce inequality and keep farming a viable industry. Such protectionism did not hinder economic growth, as is clear from history, because low inequality stimulates consumer spending and thus prevents excess production.

Balanced Trade

At the start of the growth process in 1950 Japan did not have much to export. It also lacked the raw materials needed in the production process. The yen was not an international currency at that time. Therefore, the nation was severely hampered by its shortage of foreign exchange.

Then came the Korean war in 1950. This was like a godsend to Japan's industry which was starved for raw materials. From the demands of the war, Japanese export prices soared along with the value of exports. The US army stationed in Okinawa also spent a considerable amount of dollars in Japan. Thus, in a single stroke, the Korean war relieved the foreign exchange shortage and, in fact, launched Japan on to an explosive path of development. Japan's key industries then imported that much more in raw materials and nearly doubled their output in just two or three years.

Imports played a major role in the economic miracle, but they were mostly imports of machinery and raw materials. They were thus crucial for business investment, but not for direct consumption. Because of the rising saving rate and plentiful loans provided by the government, there were sufficient funds available for domestic investment; but without new technology and raw materials, this investment would not have been undertaken.

The need for importing raw materials, plant and equipment meant that Japan suffered from constant trade deficit in its current account, which was financed by the import of foreign capital. This type of trade deficit produces high growth, because the import surplus is for investment which will increase production in the future. From that increased production will come an export surplus. Thus, today's import surplus would be matched by tomorrow's export surplus and trade would be balanced over time -- say, over one or two decades. This is the path that the United States had followed in the 19th century, and Japan duplicated it after 1950 with greater success.

In fact, after 1967 Japan began to have a surplus in its foreign trade account and rarely had deficits in the 1970s and thereafter. Foreign exchange was no longer a constraint on growth. In reality, it was never an effective constraint, because growth was still exceptional. It was merely a nagging worry that created some uncertainty in the country.

The government followed a policy of balanced trade, and periodically tried to balance its current account. Whenever, the deficit was high, the government raised interest rates to reduce investment spending and hence imports. Therefore, the policy was aimed at maintaining a balance between exports and imports. From 1950 to 1973, Japan's trade was balanced over time, as the deficits until 1967 were matched by surpluses thereafter.

Balanced Budget

From 1950 to at least 1965 the government adopted a strict policy of balanced budgets. In fact, this was stated clearly in the Finance Act of 1947 which included a clause prohibiting the issue of long term bonds to finance deficit spending. This was the country's response to severe inflation caused by the over-issue of government bonds during the war.

The Finance Act did not prohibit the issuance of bonds to finance the construction of infrastructure and other capital projects, but until 1965 even construction bonds were not issued. Thus, the government followed a strict policy of balanced budgets. In 1965, there was a major shortfall in revenue because of the recession. The government then began to issue construction bonds, but they remained small in value. By and large the government remained committed to the balanced budget principle until 1975.

The effect of this policy was that private savings went only to capital formation. The government did not use, or misuse, savings, which went into business investment. Later, when construction bonds were issued they also fostered capital formation. This way, until 1975 the government budget policy

80

essentially stimulated investment.

Yet government expenditure expanded greatly. This is because the economy grew much faster than expected. Prices also rose regularly and substantially under the impetus of expanding demand caused by soaring investment. The tax system became sharply progressive after 1954, so that tax revenue grew faster than nominal GDP. (Nominal GDP is the money value of GDP not adjusted for inflation.) That is why revenue grew briskly, faster than the nominal GDP growth of 15%. Such revenue increases enabled the government to increase spending for infrastructure and social welfare.

Increased government spending on infrastructure was a wise use of tax revenue, because it expanded social overhead capital that raises the productivity of the private sector. During the 1950s, government spending emphasized land development and flood control, but during the 1960s its focus shifted to roads and bridges. The shift was in response to the internal development of the auto industry, and as cars became popular, roads had to be built for efficient transportation.

Government spending also added to national demand, which in turn encouraged production. Since the saving rate was high and rising after 1960, even the balanced budgets greatly stimulated demand. This is because the government normally does not save money from its tax income. If taxes are cut, the public increases spending by a smaller amount, because a part of its increased after-tax income would go into increased savings.

As an example, suppose the government cuts taxes by ¥10 trillion; then under the balanced budget policy, its spending also falls by the same amount. The public now has a higher post-tax income of ¥10 trillion. If the rate of saving is 20%, then consumer spending rises only by ¥8 trillion. The tax cut policy ultimately causes a fall in national demand of ¥2 trillion. The opposite happens when taxes rise.

Thus when tax revenue rises sharply, the balanced budget policy also greatly raises national demand. The policy is even more effective in stimulating growth when the rise in revenue increases government spending on infrastructure, such as roads, bridges, airports, etc. Thus, the balanced budget policy stimulated growth in many ways.

First, it permitted the full absorption of private savings by business investment. Secondly, it increased national demand and thus supported larger output and employment. Finally, it created no deficit and debt and, therefore, no interest burden for future generations.

By contrast, a deficit budget policy followed by nations nowadays absorbs private savings, reduces investment and creates debt to be financed by future generations. A legacy of debt to the children is the worst aspect of this strategy.

Regulation Of Banks

The occupation authorities had closed a few banks that had been suspected of collaborating with the war-time military government. That left a vacuum in the financing needs of industry. Old banks were later allowed to make a comeback under different names. In 1951 the Japan Development Bank was established to supply low interest funds to key industries. Soon after that the Japan Export-Import Bank was established to promote exports. In addition, the government founded some finance corporations to provide low-cost funds to various industries. All these institutions and commercial banks were controlled by the central bank known as the Bank of Japan.

The government's financial activities expanded rapidly after

1950. Since most financial institutions needed government funds, the Bank of Japan came to exercise great control over them. This way, the government kept a tight rein on the activities of commercial banks.

During the 1950s and the 1960s Japan's stock market was not fully developed, although it had been established in the late 19th century. It had always been speculative and most people distrusted it. Instead, savers deposited their money in the government-controlled postal saving system or with commercial banks. Companies were also unable to raise funds in the stock market and they met their voracious appetite for money through commercial loans, especially from large houses known as City Banks. Because of the under-developed stock exchange, bank capital was used mostly for productive purposes.

Lending to City Banks by the Bank of Japan has become an important way of supplying funds to industry in the post-war period. The central bank regulates the supply and demand for money by adjusting its discount rate, which is the interest rate that the City Banks pay to the Bank of Japan for the loans. These loans are the most important way in which cash currency has been supplied to the private sector.

The Bank of Japan regulated the activities of commercial banks through a policy called "window guidance." The banks were told when and where to increase their loans. The discount rate and window guidance were frequently used to face the crises created by trade deficits.

Because of fast economic growth, prices rose rapidly during the era of high growth. The average inflation rate per year was 5% during 1950 to 1973. This should have raised the interest rates, but it did not. Normally, high inflation creates high interest rates, but in Japan they declined gradually from the mid-1950s until 1973. There were two reasons for this.

First, the Bank of Japan kept the discount rate low and made plentiful loans to City Banks to create rapid growth of money. Secondly, and more importantly, there were few speculative activities in the economy to waste capital. The high saving rate also provided sufficient funds to commercial banks and, in spite of the high growth rate of money that frequently exceeded 15%, limited the inflation rate to an average 5%.

The real rate of interest, i.e. the real cost of money, is the actual interest rate minus the rate of inflation. After 1955, interest rates charged by banks steadily declined and varied between 6% and 8%. With inflation at 5%, real rates of interest thus varied between 1% and 3%. These were exceptionally low rates and they played a valuable role in stimulating business investment.

Even though inflation was a persistent feature of the era of high growth, it did not hurt the economy at all. It is well known that a rapid growth of money supply is necessary to generate inflation. This was certainly true in Japan as its central bank extended plentiful credit to City Banks at a low discount rate and printed great amounts of money to finance the capital needs of industry.

As a result of high money growth, national demand was constantly ahead of national supply, thus generating a persistent upward pressure on prices. During the 1950s the annual inflation rate averaged 4%, which accelerated to 5.6% during the 1960s as money growth increased.

Between 1950 and 1973 consumer prices tripled. Yet the economy kept booming. The traditional theory is that inflation should be avoided at all costs. At most it should be around 3% per year. Anything above this level creates stagnant growth, unemployment and a worried public.

As usual, the Japanese experience defies conventional wisdom among economists. In order to clarify the argument, we should distinguish between two types of inflation: investment-driven inflation versus consumption-driven inflation.

Investment-driven inflation does not hurt and may even be desirable to raise the living standard quickly. This is what happened during the era of high growth. Rapid growth of money did generate excessive national demand, but it was led by high investment spending and capital formation. This in turn was necessary to introduce new technology, which sharply raised labor productivity in all sectors. Rising productivity in turn raised real wages because of fierce competition among firms. Thus, the living standard soared, in spite of, or perhaps because of, high money growth and inflation. In fact, as money growth and inflation accelerated during the 1960s, the living standard jumped at an even faster pace.

When economists denounce high inflation as an evil, they are really talking about consumption-driven inflation, which, of course, is a culprit in perpetuating poverty. When high money growth finances consumption, especially government consumption, it creates no productive capacity. High government consumption in turn stifles investment and capital formation, choking labor efficiency in the process. Real wages and the living standard then must decline.

The moral of the story is that investment-driven inflation, like the investment-driven trade deficit, may be good for the economy, especially when the country is catching up with the rest of the world. The era of rapid growth in Japan confirms this conclusion. Under certain circumstances, printing extra money is good for the nation.

With respect to speculation, the progressive ideal was

followed only partially. Although stock speculation was limited, land speculation was high, especially during the 1950s when the land price index soared from 55.5 in 1950 to 867 in 1960--almost a sixteen-fold jump in just ten years. In fact, land speculation was a persistent problem that continued in the 1960s and all the way until 1991.

This was a wastage of capital and if this had been avoided the living standard would have risen even faster. In spite of this wastage, the economic achievements of Japan during the period of rapid growth were very impressive--indeed miraculous. This shows the power of investment-driven policies and competitive protectionism, wherein high import barriers are combined with fierce rivalry among firms at home. The result is that companies are forced to behave efficiently because of the pressure of internal competition, but they are not decimated by low wages or a lack of environmental concerns abroad. (I have explored this concept in detail in *The Great American Deception*)

Overview

Let us now summarize our findings so far. In spite of total devastation from the Second World War and no natural resources, Japan experienced unparalleled economic growth between 1950 and 1973. Such an achievement with growth averaging 10% a year has never been duplicated by any other nation. What was the secret? The progressive, and in some way, conservative economic policies that Japan followed intentionally, or unintentionally. Regional monopolies, such as the Zaibatsu, were dissolved; some others were broken up into smaller units. All this created furious competition among the firms and industries.

86

Similarly, land ownership was transferred to tenants, and labor unions were legalized, covering some 60% of the labor force. While these measures were forced from outside, others, such as company loyalty and the lifetime employment system, evolved within Japan.

Other progressive policies were also developed from within. They included protectionism, tight control of interest rates and banks, policies of balanced trade and budgets, low inequality, and, above all, concern, though belated, for the environment. Thus, in a matter of 25 years, progressive economic policies transformed post-war Japan from the ashes of defeat into a global economic giant. The country actually became a role model for its neighbors and other third world economies seeking to eliminate poverty for their people.

Stagnation in Japan: 1975-1997

Alas, some of the progressive policies followed by Japan since the war were abandoned after 1975. Ever since then the standard of living has stagnated and signs of labor exploitation have appeared.

Reforms after the war were dictated either by General MacArthur, or by common sense. Later, as the country became prosperous, many bright young men went to prominent US universities to study economics. There they learned the virtues of deficit budgets, stock speculation, financial deregulation and company mergers. They passed these virtues on to their policy makers who followed them dutifully. These policies would turn out to be serious mistakes.

In the matter of trade policy, Japan did not adopt free trade, as advocated by US scholars, but committed a mistake anyway. It abandoned its concern for balanced trade and became interested in exports for their own sake. No longer were they needed just to import raw materials, plant and equipment. Instead, exports were considered necessary for economic growth as well. The balanced trade policy was replaced by a trade surplus policy. Slowly, but surely, Japan became dependent on foreign markets.

In the first part of its growth experience lasting until 1975, Japan needed foreign countries for raw materials. In the second part, however, the country needed foreign countries to provide raw materials as well as demand for its manufactures.

There were thus many changes in economic policy after 1975, and the era of rapid growth came to an end. Even while Japan was busy conquering world markets, its internal base grew weak. Now the country is passing through the worst crisis not only since the war, but since the Great Depression of the 1930s.

Stagnant Living Standard

To many people my statement that Japan has been more or less stagnant since 1975 will come as a surprise. After all, real GDP rose regularly till 1990, and faster than that in other G-7 countries. Japan is now a lender to the world. The country is also among the leaders in foreign aid. I am aware of all this. Still, the living standard has stagnated in Japan since 1973.

Table 7 presents data for the real wage index, national tax burden, the after-tax real wage and real per-capita GDP evaluated at 1990 prices. As far as per-capita GDP is concerned, there is still a substantial increase from 1973 to 1996.

The per-capita GDP rises from ¥2.04 million to ¥3.8 million in terms of 1990 prices. This is a growth of 86% over 23 years,

Table 7. The Real Wage Index and Real Per Capita GDP, 1973-1996 (1990 = 100)

Year	Real Wage	National Tax Burden(%)	After-Tax Real Wage	Per-Capita GDP
1973	79.4	25.0	59.5	2.04
1975	80.2	25.8	59.5	2.07
1980	85.5	31.3	58.7	2.46
1985	89.8	34.6	58.7	2.85
1990	100.0	39.6	60.4	3.40
1993	99.8	38.6	61.3	3.59
1996	100.00	37.5	62.5	3.80

Source: Same as in Table 5 plus *Statistical Abstract of the United States, 1997*

which is still high relative to that of other G-7 countries, although it pales before Japan's gains during the era of rapid growth. But if you look at the real wage, growth is just 26% over more than two decades. This comes to an average of 1.2% per year -- a far cry from the record of the first period, when the real wage climbed by more than 300%.

However, even this rise in the real wage is misleading. For most workers, especially the young and the middle-aged, the living standard is determined by their take-home salary or the after-tax real wage.

The index of the take-home wage was 59.5 in 1973 and 62.5 in 1996. It was more or less constant as taxes went up to neutralize whatever little growth occurred in the real wage. This happened even though national productivity, as measured by real per-capita GDP, rose by 86%.

Where did this productivity rise go? Since labor got little of this rise, it must have gone to government or other resource owners, such as capital and land. Since the national tax burden rose from a rate of 25.0 to 37.5, a rise of 50%, half of the productivity rise went to the government sector. The remaining half thus went to capital and land in the form of higher profits and rents. Clearly, commercial and residential rents have risen much faster than the consumer price index since 1973.

For convenience of analysis, Japan's economic experience since the war may be divided into two periods. The first, lasting between 1950 and 1975, may be called the period of balanced or progressive policies, and the second since 1975 till today, may be called the period of traditional policies.

Thus, balanced budgets gave way to deficit budgets; the balanced trade policy was replaced by a trade-surplus policy. Labor unions became weak, and the degree of competition declined through company mergers. Land speculation, which was already strong, was raised to another level through stock speculation

Banks were deregulated, which effectively raised their costs and made them prone to taking risks through speculative loans. A lot of capital was wasted during the second period as the government relaxed its control over the financial sector.

In the period of progressive policies, economic growth was exceptionally strong with after-tax real wages rising from an index of 21.1 in 1955 to 59.5 in 1973. This amounted to a rise of 182% over 18 years. National productivity, on the other hand, went up from 0.52 to 2.04, a rise of 292%. Since 182 divided by 292 equals 0.62, we may conclude that the after-tax real wage rose by 62% of the productivity rise. In other words, 62% of the productivity rise went to labor, net of taxes.

Since the tax burden rose from 20 to 25, a rise of 25%, a

90

quarter of the productivity gain went to the government, and the remaining 13% share of productivity growth went to capital and land. This means that since the income tax rate had become very progressive, the government took a big bite out of capital's income which tends to be high.

In the period of progressive policies, income inequity declined for two reasons. One was the decline in the wage differentials between small and large firms. The other was the rising portion of government spending on social welfare in the mid-1960s and thereafter.

In the second period, productivity rose by 86%, but the after-tax real wage was more or less constant. The wage index declined a bit till 1985 and then rose slowly till 1996. With wage stagnation also came a rise in the wage differential and the resulting inequality. The progressive tax system, however, kept the inequality rise under check.

As stated earlier, the government absorbed about half of the rise in productivity, with the rest going to capital and other factors. Corporate profits went up sharply, especially from 1975 to 1985, when the after-tax wages declined a little. (See Kurokawa Toshio, p.145) Moreover, because of high rates of depreciation permitted by law, the rise in internal cash reserves was much larger than reported profits.

Company mergers began to occur in the 1960s, but increased sharply during the 1970s. As a result, industrial concentration that had been falling in the 1950s till the mid-1960s began to rise thereafter. The concentration ratios in different industries slowly approached the US levels. This ratio is the market share in an industry controlled by the top three firms. These ratios increased in many industries during the 1970s and high competition gave way to giant oligopolistic firms.

While the change did not significantly hurt the competitive

pressure among various firms, it weakened the unions to the extent that they were unable to secure wage gains in proportion to their efficiency gains. Japanese firms were still very competitive with respect to those in other countries, but labor bargaining suffered in the process. This is the main reason why the after-tax real wage failed to rise, in spite of still respectable rises in national productivity. Clearly, the degree of economic democracy in factories had suffered.

We may, thus, conclude that as far as the take-home salary is concerned, the Japanese economy has been at a standstill since 1975. Since the after-tax real wage is the best measure of the living standard, Japan has been in stagnation ever since that year. Today, Japan is facing a serious crisis with declining employment and real incomes, but the roots of this crisis can be traced far back to several changes that occurred in the 1970s. Some of these changes, such as the oil shock of 1973, were beyond the nation's control, but many others were policy mistakes. Let us now see how these policies evolved in the 1970s.

Budget Deficits

The central government's budgets were balanced until 1965. The Finance Act of 1947 had permitted the issuance of construction bonds to finance public investment in the social overhead capital, but even these bonds were not issued. Until 1965 the budget policy was one of strict balance.

From 1965 to 1974, construction bonds were indeed issued to finance deficit spending, but they were small and their purpose was to foster capital formation in the private sector through improvements in the country's infrastructure. Strictly speaking, construction bonds did not constitute deficit

92

financing in the legal sense. Nor did they represent a government policy of deficit budgets. (See Takofoshi Ito, p.165 for this view)

The real deficit budget policy where government spending rises sharply to fight unemployment began in 1975. That year, deficit-financing bonds or "deficit-bonds," as they are often called, were issued for the first time in post-war Japan. For this reason, 1975 was a watershed year and it was a clear departure from the progressive policy of balanced budgets.

At first, the government regarded the issuance of these bonds as temporary and the budgets were to be balanced again as soon as possible, but definitely by 1980. However, the deficit actually increased in 1980 and persisted till 1997.

The budget deficit as a percentage of GDP stood at 0.5% in 1970. In 1975, it jumped to 3.5% and slowly rose thereafter until the peak of 6% in 1979. After that, the deficit ratio steadily declined and reached a low of 1.3% in 1990. No deficit bonds were issued that year. However, that was only a temporary halt. At the end of 1995, the deficit ratio, based on local and central government bond issues, had soared to 7.5%.

From 1975 to 1990 the average deficit ratio was 4%, which was higher than the average deficit ratio of 3.7% in the United States in the same period. In terms of budget deficits, the United States has been regarded as the ring leader in the world. But if we compare deficit ratios, Japan is way ahead ahead of America.

In fairness, it must be mentioned that US deficits were mostly consumption-driven, whereas, even after 1975, Japanese deficits had a small investment component. But beating America in this respect shows how sharply the attitudes had changed in Japan towards deficit spending. Japan's policy was now guided by American scholars who recommended deficit financing as a way to combat unemployment.

Sometimes this policy works, sometimes it does not. It is all a matter of supply and demand. When national supply is less than national demand, deficit financing greatly raises prices and adds to inflation. Such was the case in the 1970s, where a big jump in oil prices had caused a sharp fall in national supply. Fighting unemployment through deficit bonds at that time was a clear mistake. But this was the policy recommended by US experts and their Japanese students, and both countries paid heavily for their errors.

Deficit financing becomes effective when national demand is less than national supply, because then inflation remains under control. But even there, bonds should not be issued, because the government has to pay interest on them. Instead, more money should be printed to finance the budget deficit.

Bond financing of deficits creates a permanent problem for future generations while solving a crisis that is only temporary in nature. That is why in 1988 more than 20% of the budget went into interest payments in Japan, compared to 15% in the United States. Both countries had by then accumulated huge debts from their bond issues in the past, but the burden was higher in Japan relative to its GDP. Even though interest rates have declined sharply in the 1990s, the current interest burden is still large.

Unbalanced Trade

Another departure from the first period of growth was the government's policy of balanced trade. Japan had suffered constant, but small, trade deficits until 1967. These were investment-driven deficits that created new high paying jobs

94

and expanded productive capacity. This in turn created export surpluses after 1967 to pay for earlier import surpluses.

While small trade deficits were common the government policy was to keep them under control. The policy itself was one of balanced trade. Whenever the trade shortfall rose sharply, the Bank of Japan raised interest rates, lowered the growth of money, and hence national demand, to bring the deficit down. Thus, even though the deficits were persistent until 1967, the government policy itself was to bring them down and maintain balanced trade. After 1975 this policy changed completely.

From 1968 to 1972 the current account of foreign trade showed a rising surplus. Thereafter, the rise in the oil price created a deficit until 1975. Between 1975 and 1997 the current account was in the negative only twice, in 1979 and 1980. Therefore, 1975 is a watershed year in terms of trade direction and policy as well.

The rising trade surplus since 1967, especially with the United States, became an international issue by 1970, because it led to a great outflow of dollars. It became more and more difficult to maintain the old exchange rate of 360 yen to the dollar. In the interest of balanced trade, the yen should have been revalued upwards, but the Japanese government resisted this policy. The entire nation had acquired a deep-seated memory of how foreign exchange shortages in the past had constrained the rate of growth and resulted in higher interest rates to limit expansion.

Even though industrialization had completely transformed the country from total demoralization after the war into a manufacturing giant, Japan continued to believe in its vulnerability to outer shocks. This belief was reinforced by the jolt of oil prices in 1973, even though Japan withstood that jolt better than any other country. Thus, a deep-seated attitude had gained roots in the Japanese mind, namely exports had to be maintained and increased at all costs. Even today, this myth stands in the way of rational policy.

Under US pressure, the yen was revalued to 308 per dollar in December 1971. Japan accepted it reluctantly under the threat of a US import surcharge. This, however, did not solve the problem of the rising trade surplus. The US pressure continued, and finally the world abandoned the fixed exchange standard and adopted a flexible rate. In 1973 the yen was revalued again and started the new regime from a value of ¥265. The oil shock, however, changed it back to ¥300 to the dollar in 1975. Thereafter Japan's exports resumed their climb and the exchange rate never saw the ¥300 mark again.

The economic crisis between 1973 and 1975 convinced the policy makers that future growth would have to come from exports. Instead of expanding the domestic demand base as they had done in the first period of growth, they now turned to overseas demand.

The Bank of Japan periodically intervened in the foreign exchange market to restrain the rise of the yen that threatened Japanese exports. Balanced trade policy required a steep rise in the international currency value of the yen; but the Bank of Japan did not permit this. This policy, in fact, further worsened the problem of inflation.

As the yen rises, the prices of foreign goods decline in Japan. If the yen had been allowed to appreciate freely, foreign oil and other raw materials would have become cheap enough to control the growth of prices. With inflation under control, rapid growth would have resumed automatically, because the rate of investment was actually higher in the 1970s. As long as investment is high, growth has to be large.

Instead, the government chose to fight unemployment with deficit bonds and intervention in the foreign exchange market. The result was that even though the rate of investment rose in the 1970s, real GDP growth fell.

The intervention in the foreign exchange market only slowed the appreciation of the yen. But so obsessed were the companies and the government with exports that they persuaded the unions to limit their wage demands during spring offensives. This was the only way to out-compete other companies in global markets and raise exports in the face of the appreciating yen.

If the yen rises, then the only way to raise exports is to lower your own prices, for which it is necessary to keep wage gains far below productivity gains. Thus, the desire of the government and companies to raise the export surplus in the face of an appreciating yen caused an ever increasing gap between real wages and labor productivity. Of course, labor unions had to be weak to accept this verdict.

The policy of trade surplus limited real wage growth. At the same time, the policy of budget deficits and the resulting tax increase reduced these limited gains to zero. Both these policies also created an unbalanced economy. As Nakamura describes it aptly: "During the high growth period domestic demand alone set the stage for 10 percent growth, ... while exports and imports roughly cancelled each other. From 1975 to 1985, however, approximately one fourth of economic growth was sustained by overseas demand." (p.115)

In 1976 Japan's trade surplus was $3.7 billion. By 1985 it had grown to $49 billion. The growing surplus meant a growing gap between domestic supply and demand. Thus, Japan became increasingly dependent on foreign markets and on the stability of its exchange rate.

The policy of trade surplus not only limited real wage gains, it also increased Japan's vulnerability to developments in foreign countries. This was an ironic development, because it was the historic fear of vulnerability that had initially motivated the government to rely on its trade surplus policy. The stress on exports at all cost actually increased this dependence.

In 1985 the yen began to climb again under the Plaza Accord that the G-7 countries had reached to bring the dollar down. Japanese companies were by now so dependent on their overseas markets that they reduced their prices again to limit the damage of yet another dose of yen appreciation. As a result, even though the yen rate rose by 100 points from 238 in 1985 to 138 in 1989, the trade surplus was still as high as $57 billion. In 1995, the surplus hit an all- time record, when it reached $130 billion. After that the trade imbalance fell slowly, but the dollar began to appreciate in 1997. This is likely to raise exports and trim imports again.

Land Prices And Housing

Nearly 70% of the land in Japan is covered by mountains and forests, so that even though the total area itself is reasonably large, the habitable area is severely limited. Land is extremely scarce and because of expanding demand from housing and industries, the price of land has risen steadily and sharply since the war.

There was a long-held belief that regardless of wars, famines or depressions, land prices in Japan move only in one direction--upward. This faith, of course, has been ruthlessly shattered since 1991. By the end of 1995 land prices in large cities had fallen by half. The unthinkable has happened.

The question arises: why was the fall in the land price unthinkable? The answer lies in history. The land price index, which was equal to 1 in 1936, rose to 2 in 1945, to 55 in 1950, to 867 in 1960, to 4,318 in 1970, to 10,000 in 1980, all the way to its peak in 1991 at 20,928. From 1 to 20,928 - such was the land price inflation in Japan in just 55 years. No wonder, people believed in the infallibility of their land investments.

However, this should also show that the laws of markets cannot be suppressed for ever. When an asset rises so fast in value, there is clearly enormous imbalance in that market. Evidently, land was an object of ceaseless speculation for more than half a century. Such speculation was rampant, even during the period of progressive policies. Banks at all levels vied with each other to lend money against land as collateral. After all, land does not depreciate. It only goes up in price. How can anybody go wrong?

With land so expensive, house prices must go up. At its peak in 1990, the average cost of an apartment in Tokyo was ¥100 million. According to John Woronoff, a correspondent at *Asian Business*: "A really nice house by Japanese standards, but no big deal by foreign ones, could easily run into ¥500 million. Something even foreigners would regard as grand might cost ¥2 billion." (p.129)

At such monstrous prices, few can afford to buy a house in Tokyo. In 1990 the average cost of a residence in Japan was 5.7 times the annual income, whereas in Tokyo it was 8.7 times. This compares with 3.4 times in the United States and 4.6 times in Germany. As a result, it should not be a surprise that the per-capita floor space in houses in other countries is much higher than that in Japan.

House prices have been rising faster than the consumer price index since the 1950s. As a result, the percentage of home ownership among people has also been falling since then. In 1958, 71.2% of families owned their homes. This figure dropped to 59.2% by 1973. It was more or less unchanged in 1995 when it stood at 60%.

Among the G-7 countries Japan has the highest rate of savings, after Italy, the lowest rate of dwelling space and the highest cost of homes. There is a connection between the home cost and the saving rate. In the United States, by contrast, homes are the cheapest, the dwelling space the highest and the saving rate the lowest.

Home ownership and consumption opportunities go together. When a person buys a house, he also needs refrigerators, carpets, furniture, air conditioners, dishwashers, paintings, among many other things. Home ownership, therefore, creates demand for many other products. Where home ownership is high, consumption is bound to be high or savings are bound to be low.

The demand for home appliances rises with the size of the living area. Larger houses need more furniture, larger refrigerators and bigger carpets, and so on. Thus, the United States has the lowest home costs, the largest dwelling space and, hence, the lowest rate of saving. By contrast, Japan has the highest home costs, the smallest dwelling space and, therefore, one of the largest rates of saving among the G-7 countries.

The high rate of saving in turn generates low consumption and, hence, low national demand. This way, the gap between supply and demand grows in nations where housing is unaffordable. This is one reason why an economy should provide affordable housing, which opens up consumption opportunities and, thus, provides an adequate demand base for high production and low unemployment.

100

In Japan, houses were not affordable, even during the first half of its growth 'experience when the nation adopted many other progressive policies. But at that time high land prices did not hurt. There was so much pent-up demand for hundreds of other things. The nation was practically starving after the war. Thus, in the first period of its growth, high home prices did not hinder development. People had yet to buy cameras, watches, appliances, cars, bicycles, motor cycles, tractors, and so on. Demand was plentiful and consumption opportunities vast, in spite of rising home cost.

Affordable housing in the first period perhaps would not have raised the growth rate, which was constrained by the shortage of foreign exchange. Only a larger supply of dollars could have stimulated higher growth, which was extraordinary any way.

However, after 1975 there was little pent-up demand for gadgets and appliances, and further increases in demand depended on larger and affordable homes. Rising land and house prices now began to hurt. To lower the rate of saving, it was now necessary to increase home ownership. This should have been the main priority of the government. Instead, the opposite continued to happen. Land and houses became more and more expensive. Even though the government expanded its residential investment, the home ownership rate remained constant at a low rate.

New housing starts even fell after 1987 and continued to fall in the 1990s. A survey of G-7 countries shows that affordable homes generate high consumption and thus low savings. This is what Japan needs the most to create a high demand base at home. High home prices did not matter in the era of progressive policies, but now they are definitely choking domestic demand, not only for houses and construction industry, but also for all other products connected to home ownership.

Financial Deregulation

A new feature of the economy emerging after the mid-1970s was financial deregulation, under which the government steadily removed controls on banks and permitted them and the securities industry to develop new products. There were two reasons for this change. One was the issuance of deficit bonds since 1975 and the other was growing pressure on Japan from US scholars and government to introduce financial innovations similar to those introduced in the American financial markets.

The banking and securities industries were always under the strict control of the Ministry of Finance. Both of them had to get a licence for operations and opening new branches. Interest rates were not free to move in accordance with credit market conditions. There were ceilings on interest rates paid on deposits. Prices of government bond issues were strictly controlled. Overseas investments by banks, insurance companies and stock brokers were also limited. In short, the financial sector had been under a tight leash in the era of progressive policies.

The purpose of all these rules was to keep interest rates low, except in emergencies created by trade deficits, when temporarily the rates would go up to reduce investment spending. The policy of low interest rates required that there was no wastage of capital by banks and other financial institutions in stock market speculation. Interest rates on deposits were also kept low for this purpose.

Such policies had originated in the aftermath of the stock

102

market crashes around the world in 1929 and in the early 1930s. Speculative bubbles had then burst in nation after nation to start the Great Depression. That is when the governments decided to impose strict controls on interest rates and financial institutions. These institutions deal with other people's money, not their own, and there is great temptation to make reckless investments.

The painful lessons of the 1930s were forgotten during the late 1970s. The US government began to remove the financial controls in 1977. The pace of such deregulation accelerated in 1979 and thereafter. In the process, many new products were created to attract the savers into banks and the stock and bond markets. Some of these were designed to increase savings. Others, such as options, interest rate futures, stock index related investments, among many others, tempted people to gamble their savings into risky investments where the potential for profit or loss was high. This was the return of the 1920s, where gambling and investing became the same.

With the issuance of deficit bonds in Japan after 1974, it was difficult to control bond prices. The size of the government debt was large, and continued borrowing by the government made it necessary to develop a market for its bonds. In the late 1970s, bond prices began to be determined in the market. In other words, interest rates, which move opposite to bond prices, began to fluctuate. Thus, long term interest rates had to be deregulated.

As Japan accumulated dollars from its surplus trade, controls were lifted on overseas investment. Furthermore, under increasing pressure from the United States, the Tokyo Stock Exchange introduced new financial products that had already found their way into the New York Stock Exchange. After 1985 even short term interest rates were deregulated. As in America, Japanese banks were allowed to pay higher interest rates on various accounts.

Between 1975 and 1985, therefore, the financial industry changed drastically. These changes laid the foundation for the subsequent bubble economy. They had two main effects. First, they lured people, companies and financial institutions into the stock market that offered a large variety of new instruments or temptations. Secondly, they raised the cost of deposits for the banks. Both these effects, along with the ever-present land speculation, generated an economic bubble that kept growing until the end of 1989.

The Bubble Economy

Land speculation had been a profitable activity for banks, corporations and individuals ever since the end of the war. In a land-scarce economy, the banks were always eager to lend money against land as collateral. In order to control property inflation, a huge capital gains tax was imposed on the transfer or sale of land in 1974. The idea was to discourage speculation, and it worked for one year as prices fell in 1975. From the next year, however, they resumed their upward march.

The capital gains tax had the intended consequences, as it discouraged the sale of land. But with few sellers around, land prices could not be contained for long. The tax also encouraged stock speculation. Instead of selling land, land owners increasingly borrowed money against their valuable holdings and put the money into company shares. For gamblers and profiteers, the capital gains tax had taken the fun out of the land market, and they turned their attention into the rapidly developing stock exchange.

The Nikkei stock index stood at 4,358 at the end of 1975. By the end of 1980 it had jumped to 7,116. The huge oil price rise in 1979 did nothing to cool the enthusiasm of the stock investor. By the end of 1985 the Nikkei climbed to 13,113. In ten years share prices had tripled. Some people had earned enormous profits from their stock investments.

This was the era of quick profits and easy money. Multi-millionaires had emerged overnight. There was now no limit to greed and ambition. Prices could not fall, so believed the people, not just for land, but also for stocks.

More fun was yet to come. America was increasingly uncomfortable with its trade deficit and Japan's trade surplus. Under the Plaza Accord, the yen resumed its historic rise. To cushion the blow of the rising yen and under US pressure, the Bank of Japan reduced the official discount rate, (ODR) , and pumped more money into the economy. Interest rates fell in 1986, even though deregulation raised the cost of funds to banks.

Banks were happy to subsidize their loans because they could raise money in the share market by issuing new stock at practically no cost. Deposit costs, indeed, had risen, but there was an another almost limitless source of funds available to them -- the ever-growing Tokyo exchange.

The rise in banking cost is also why banks turned increasingly to the stock market. It forced the banks to seek a higher return to compensate for increasing costs, and the higher return was easily available from soaring stock prices. Thus, the deregulation of interest rates was partially responsible for inflating the share market bubble, just as it had done in the world in the 1920s.

Those who made money from stocks spent their profits on land. This way, land prices soared with the soaring stock market. Landowners increased their borrowing against their high valued collateral, and put this money again into stocks. This way, rising prices in one market supported prices in the other. And the race was on. The land market supported the stock market and the stock market supported the land market, in an ever expanding bubble. The sky was the limit over these prices.

In this background the Bank of Japan, for some reason, continued to lower its discount rate. This was like adding fuel to fire. Lower interest rates only inflated the bubble.

Low interest rates and the asset price boom sparked an investment boom. Companies spent money on new plant and equipment as if they were in the 1950s, when there was no limit to domestic demand. GDP growth soared; so did the bubble.

Deregulation of the financial markets, in fact, had sparked a global bubble in share prices. It was in this frenzied atmosphere that my book, *The Great Depression of 1990*, made its appearance. I had warned about a stock market crash, possibly at the end of 1987 and then at the end of 1989.

On October 19th, 1987 markets crashed around the globe, stunning everybody in the process. In Japan, however, the panic was short-lived. Within six months, share prices completely recovered, with no end in sight.

The Nikkei index had ended at the level of 13,113 in 1985. By the end of 1989, it reached 38,916. In the decade after 1975 the stock index had tripled. After 1985 it tripled again in just four years. Money supply grew by 52% over these years and much of this growth went into the asset markets.

However, it was clear by the middle of 1989 that the bubble party would soon be over. The Bank of Japan, worried by spiralling asset prices, had begun to raise the discount rate.

Yet no one took this small rise seriously. The discount rate rose again. Drunk with the success of quick profits, again no one noticed.

 At the end of 1989, an unusually sharp cold spell around the world suddenly raised the price of oil. This, along with rising interest rates, pricked the stock market bubble, and share prices began to fall from the first trading day in 1990. Surprisingly, the land bubble continued to inflate. It was only after the Bank of Japan imposed strict controls on bank lending against land, that the land bubble also burst in September 1990. The bubble economy has been in crisis ever since.

Conclusion

A series of progressive policies had been adopted by Japan from 1950 to 1973 and they created the era of rapid growth, averaging 10%. During this period, real wages rose sharply, both before and after taxes, income inequality fell, the economy diversified, and Japan emerged as a global economic power. The progressive policies that had been followed were balanced budgets, balanced trade, tight regulation of banks, high domestic competition but little foreign competition, land reform and lifetime employment.

However, after 1975 these policies were abandoned one by one. Budgets were no longer balanced, balanced trade gave way to surplus trade, banks were deregulated, high competition gave way to oligopolistic industries with strong control over unions, and income inequality was allowed to rise. As a result, in spite of respectable economic growth and productivity rise, the living standard of the vast majority of the Japanese people remained constant. In addition, huge imbalances appeared in major markets for land, stocks, property, foreign trade, and housing, among many others. The combined name for all these imbalances is the Bubble Economy, which burst at the start of 1990.

A recession began officially in April 1991 and the economy showed few signs of revival even at the end of 1997. In fact, the country suffered the worst crisis in terms of unemployment, bank failures, corporate bankruptcies, budget deficits and debt since the last great depression in the 1930s. It is clear that the cure lies in the progressive policies that had transformed Japan into a global economic giant in just 25 years--policies that were abandoned later under the influence of US-trained scholars and emotional attachment to exports.

The sad part is that the living standard stagnated after 1975, while productivity continued to rise. This happened in spite of the same old sacrifices made by the people in terms of high savings and long working hours. And today the country stands in danger of chaos and depression.

* * *

4. Global Speculative

Bubbles

The twentieth century is unique in that it has witnessed a number of speculative bubbles around the world in stock as well as real estate markets. Every bubble has burst in the end. Some have lasted for more than a decade, some for less, but every balloon was eventually punctured either by an unexpected global event or by the internal dynamics of market forces.

Some people call today's economy an information economy, where the flow of data and charts is swift and voluminous.

Computers, fax machines, telephones, and jets, have linked the planet in a vast chain of communications that is constantly on the move. One wonders why bubbles are born at all in a world where information is so readily available. Don't the speculators know that, without exception, every bubble has burst in the past? Don't they know that once you ride a tiger, it is very difficult, nay impossible, to get off its back without injury or worse?

Since bubbles keep recurring in our history, there must be something in human nature and institutions that generates them inevitably. If the bursting of a bubble were not painful, one could neglect its underlying causes. But few bubbles have been benign; when they puncture, they leave a long trail of bankruptcies, broken homes, unemployment, crime and starvation. Not just the speculators but the whole society then suffers with them. That is why speculative bubbles should be nipped in the bud, before they get out of control.

The Bubble of the 1920s

The first speculative bubble of this century occurred in America in the 1920s. It is often the case that an inflationary boom in one asset sparks a similar boom in some other assets as well. Normally, when share prices jump, the value of real estate, and sometime art objects, also climbs. In the bubble of the 1920s, share prices soared along with real estate in some parts of the United States, especially Florida. Profits from stock market gains were invested in the property sector and vice versa.

The property bubble burst in 1926, but the share bubble continued till October 1929, when it too punctured to start an unprecedented global depression. Figure 1 displays the behavior of the Dow Jones Index in the 1920s and the early 1930s. The Dow jumped from 72 in 1920 to 360 by October 1929, and then began to crash. By the end of 1933, it had

Figure 1

Stock Price Index in the United States: 1920-1934

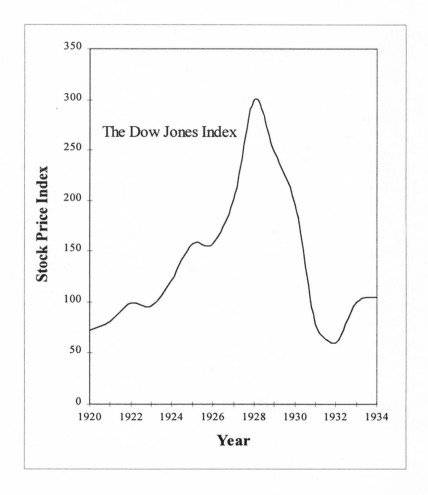

Source: P. S. Pierce, *The Dow Jones Averages: 1885-1990*

111

plummeted to 60 or by over 80 percent. It was just about back to where it had started in 1920.

The Japanese Bubble

The stock bubble of the 1920s lasted, with a few minor interruptions, the whole decade. A similar bubble began in Japan in the mid-1970s and endured for a full fifteen years before it came to a halt and collapsed. We have studied its behavior before, and a brief mention is desirable again for comparison.

Figure 2 tracks the course of the Nikkei index from 1975 to 1985 and then to 1989 and beyond; the index tripled in the first phase, and then tripled again in the second phase. This was perhaps the longest and the fattest bubble in history, which began to burst at the start of 1990. Both share prices and real estate values crashed at that time, and fell intermittently for two years; then they remained more or less stable and recovered. In 1997, Japan's share prices began their free fall again, and the Nikkei index plunged more than 20% for the year, hitting a low of 15,082 on November 14th.

Interestingly, as with the United States in the 1920s, the Japanese bubble of the 1970s and the 1980s combined stock inflation with property inflation. The two fed on each other, as the world first watched with amazement and then denounced what until then was the worst speculative mania in history.

The US Bubble: 1982-1997

The Japanese bubble lasted from 1975 to 1989 and then crashed in 1990. A similar US bubble began in 1982 and was still continuing at the end of November 1997. In the recession of the early 1980s, the Dow hit a low of 804 in June 1982 and then began to climb, as the Federal Reserve System (the Fed) began to trim short-term interest rates in order to fight the

112

Figure 2

Stock Price Index in Japan: 1975-1997

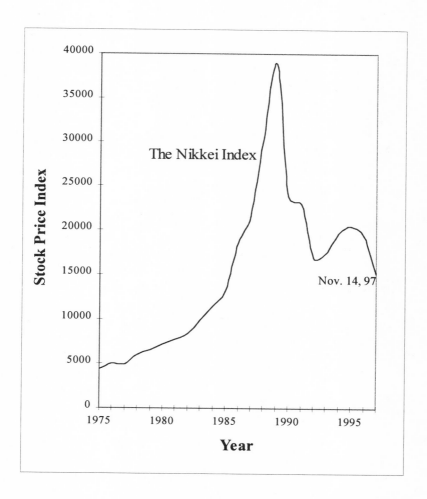

Source: *Economic Statistic Annual*, Bank of Japan

113

Figure 3

Stock Price Index in the United States: 1982-1997

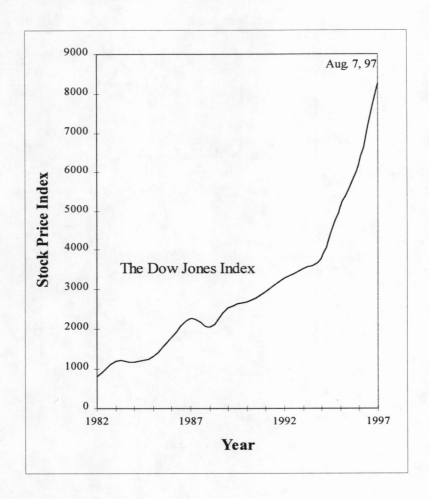

Source: *Economic Report of the President*, various issues

114

economic slump. Falling rates of interest stimulate stock prices for several reasons.

First, other financial instruments such as bonds become less attractive because of their lower yield. Second, business investment grows because of the reduced cost of borrowed money that can be used to finance capital projects. Third, declining interest rates induce people to buy new homes and appliances that many people buy on credit, thereby spurring the economy and eventually corporate profits. Finally, low borrowing costs may encourage speculation as people invest their borrowed funds into the stock or property market. Speculation rises especially when a lot of new instruments, such as options and other derivatives, become available in asset markets.

The US bubble started in 1982 and slowly inflated until 1986. At the beginning of 1987, it began to balloon, with the Dow rising from around 1900 to its hitherto peak on August 25 at 2722, or a hefty 43% in just eight months. Compare this with the long-term gain in the Dow of about 10% per year. In one week in the month of October, from the 12th to the 16th, the stock-price index fell 9.5 percent; the following Monday on October 19th it plummeted 508 points or 22.6%, all the way down to 1738. This was the largest single fall since 1929, in both absolute and percentage terms.

Black Monday shook markets around the world, including the one sizzling in Tokyo. The next day, the Nikkei index tumbled 15%. Did the worst-ever stock market crash of 1987 stop the speculative fever? Yes, but only for a few months. In 1988, bubbles began to inflate again, slowly in America but vigorously in Japan. Wall Street experts and scholars denounced the Japanese financial institutions for fear of the repeat of the October massacre in 1987. But the pundits in Tokyo defended their practices and asserted that Japan was different and immune to an enduring slump. They declared the 1987 debacle to be a minor anomaly that in any case did not and could not last long in a country that had been growing strong ever since 1950. No one in Japan believes in this rhetoric anymore: nations, like people, have to learn from their own experience.

In the United States, share prices continued their positive trend until August 1990, when oil prices rose sharply because of Iraq's invasion of the oil-rich kingdom of Kuwait. But following Iraq's crushing defeat in the Gulf War in January next year, the Dow resumed its climb, this time out of all proportion.

The stock index was at 2600 at the beginning of 1991; by August 7, 1997, it hit an all-time high of 8259, rocketing by more than 10 times the low of 804 reached 15 years ago in June 1982. In Japan, the Nikkei had climbed from 4358 in 1975 to 38,916 on the last day of 1989. This was a jump of 793 percent, but the US bubble even excelled that of the Tokyo stock exchange. From trough to peak, the Dow had soared 927 percent. No wonder, the New York Stock Exchange, the home of the Dow, is said to have witnessed a market of the millennium.

Wall Street Fundamentals

What was behind such an unprecedented surge? Wall Street pundits in New York have offered a variety of explanations, even though none of them ever foresaw the share mania of the 1980s and the 1990s. As for myself, I had at least foreseen the market jump of the 1980s in *The Great Depression of 1990*, and even anticipated the possibility of a severe contraction by the end of 1987. In Japan, of course, the stock market crashed in 1990 and a long slump began. As shown later, the collapse of the Nikkei index set in motion a long chain of events that finally led to the currency crisis and stock market crashes in 1997.

116

Thus 1990 turned out to be a pivotal year that first crippled Japan, the second largest economy in the world, and then set the stage for a possible world-wide collapse, beginning seven years later in 1997. In *The Great American Deception*, I listed 30 forecasts that I have made since 1978, and two of them did not materialize on time. I think those two will come true in 1998 and 1999.

Soon after Black Monday, I, along with a financial analyst, Andrew Tobias, appeared on the Donahue Show. I told Mr. Tobias that the Dow could reach 4,000 and then crash, and Mr. Tobias dutifully reported our conversation in the next month's issue of *Money* magazine.

Frankly, I never foresaw the share mania of the 1990s; nor did anyone else, although in my 1978 work, *The Downfall of Capitalism and Communism*, I had argued that something would happen before the year 2000 that would turn Americans vehemently against the dominant class of the wealthy. As discussed in chapter 6, this could happen in 1998 and the reason would be a series of stock market crashes.

Wall Street pundits argued that this time around it was different, something reminiscent of the constant earlier refrain that Japan was different. Financial analysts and brokers, frequently heard on money shows on CNN, CNBC and other business-related TV programs, along with the writers in popular newspapers and politicians basking for years in the glow of the soaring Dow, agreed on one single point: this time the fundamentals were sound. In other words, the share manias of the past were admittedly irrational, because they were not backed by a strong economy. But this time things were entirely different. What were those fundamentals on which most experts concurred?

One mantra that I heard again and again was that we now have low inflation, low interest rates and low unemployment, a combination that has not occurred since the mid-1960s. Were the pundits lying? No. The 30-year US Treasury bond yielded a puny 6 percent at the end of 1997; the inflation rate was just 2.5 percent and the unemployment rate was below 5 percent. No, they were not lying. The information was correct, but it was misinformation nevertheless.

Not a single analyst reminded the public of 1929, when inflation was at zero, the bond yield at 4 percent and unemployment at 3 percent. In terms of the so-called Wall Street fundamentals, the fateful year of 1929 was infinitely better. Yet the stock market crashed and the Great Depression began. I will describe the true economic fundamentals in the next chapter.

Bubbles in the Asian Tigers

Globalization of the world economy has linked the markets for goods, services and assets. In conjunction with the bubbles in Japan and the United States sprang bubbles all across the planet. They are described by charts presented in the appendix, as a picture is worth a thousand words.

Because of data problems, the charts cover only the period 1987 to 1996, even though the speculative mania began around the world in 1982. Japan's stock surge, of course, started much earlier, but it was not accompanied by a similar surge in other large economies. Japan's mania also ended early, while in some other parts of the world, the mania continued well into 1997. In what follows, unless otherwise specified, the share market behavior of a country is described in terms of the local currency only.

As elsewhere, share bubbles in the economies of the little tigers--South Korea, Hong Kong, Singapore and Taiwan-- resumed in 1988. In Korea, the share market reached its peak in 1994, rising by 81% in seven years, when measured either in terms of the local currency, the won, or in terms of the US dollar. Thereafter, the market declined because of the

Figure 4

Stock-Price Index In South Korea: 1987-96

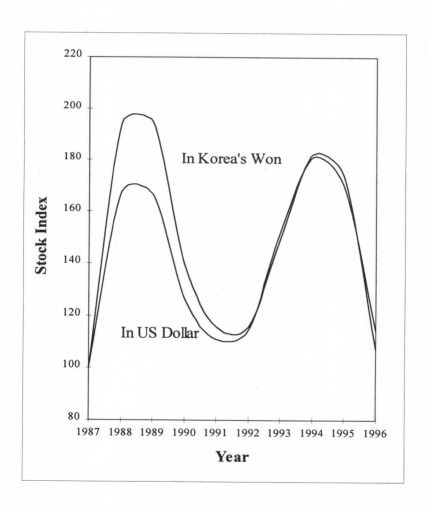

Source: Morgan Stanley Capital International

119

rising trade deficit. The Korean market surge actually lasted one year, 1988, during which it soared 67 percent. Thereafter, the market declined because of the rising trade deficit. In 1990, it limped along, and a long negative trend began in 1991.

In Taiwan, share prices soared in 1988 and 1989, rising 264 percent in just two years. Thereafter, they collapsed, tumbling 63 percent by 1992, before resuming their surge of 128 percent by 1996. Taiwan's markets are notorious for their volatility; nevertheless, share prices rose 204 percent in the nine years between 1987 to 1996.

In Hong Kong, where the market is also as unpredictable as in Taiwan, share prices jumped 400 percent between 1987 and 1993. Then they crashed over the next two years, before recovering fully in 1996 and reaching an all-time high in July 1997. Overall, stock values had climbed by 426 percent between 1987 and 1996, clearly qualifying to be a part of the global speculative bubble.

In Singapore, in terms of the local dollar, share prices jumped by 173 percent between 1987 and 1993, about an average of 29 percent per year. But in terms of the US dollar, the jump was much larger at 257 percent. This is a reflection of the long-term weakness of the US dollar in world markets, especially after 1985. Following 1993, the local currency share prices began a negative trend that has yet to reverse itself.

It is clear that the little tigers, except for Hong Kong, have not experienced the kind of bubble that the United States has seen in the 1990s, although their stocks have been highly volatile. However, Hong Kong, with its dollar linked to the American currency, was in the midst of a speculative bubble until the middle of 1997, and markets in Taiwan and Singapore were still far above their 1987 level.

* * *

Figure 5

Stock-Price Index In Taiwan: 1987-96

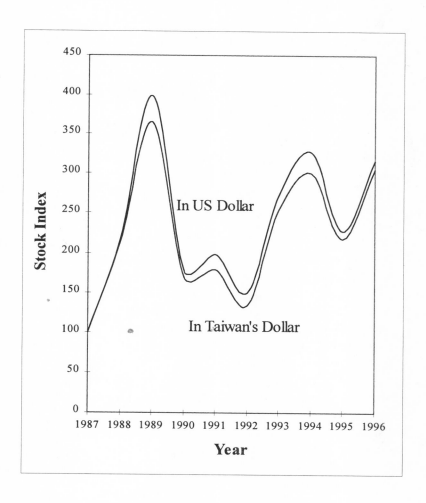

Source: Morgan Stanley Capital International

Figure 6

Stock-Price Index In Hong Kong: 1987-96

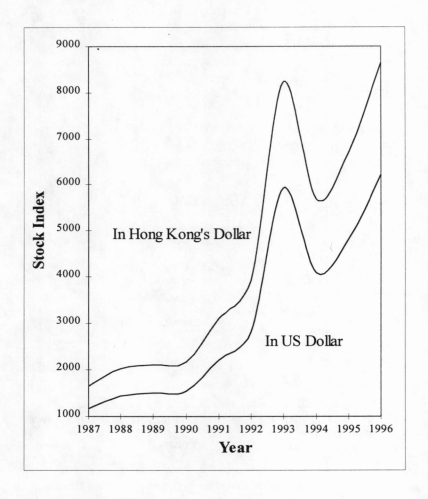

Source: Morgan Stanley Capital International

Bubbles in the Baby Tigers

The economies of the baby tigers, though flourishing for decades, are much smaller than those of their neighbors, and therefore more prone to share price volatility. Between 1987 to 1996, Indonesia saw its stock index jump by 812 percent in terms of the Rupiah and by 408 percent in terms of the US dollar. This is an impressive performance by any measure. The country did suffer a crash in 1991 when the price of oil, which Indonesia exports, plunged; but the markets staged a quick recovery thereafter.

Malaysian stocks climbed by over 330 percent in terms of the Ringgit and the US dollar between 1987 and 1996. But the peak, as in Singapore, occurred in 1993, before share prices recovered by the end of 1996.

The Filipino markets tell much the same story. Between 1987 and 1996, stocks priced in terms of the local currency jumped 544 percent, but the peak had occurred in 1993. The jump was also impressive in terms of the US dollar.

In Thailand also, share prices reached their zenith in 1993, but then crashed never to recover again. Nevertheless, Thai stocks had gained over 220 percent in terms of local and American currencies between 1987 and 1996.

It is clear that share markets among all the tigers except Korea have been entangled with the global bubble although in their own volatile way. By the middle of 1997, most of these markets had shed some of their gains, but were still highly inflated compared to the trough reached at the end of 1987.

Europe's Bubble

Western Europe had its own bubble that paralleled the trend in the United States. Historically, events in Europe and America

123

Figure 7

Stock-Price Index In France: 1987-97

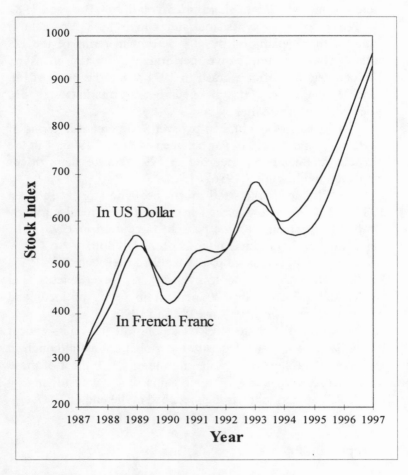

Source: Morgan Stanley Capital International and
        MEI Indicators, OECD

Figure 8

Stock-Price Index In Britain: 1987-97

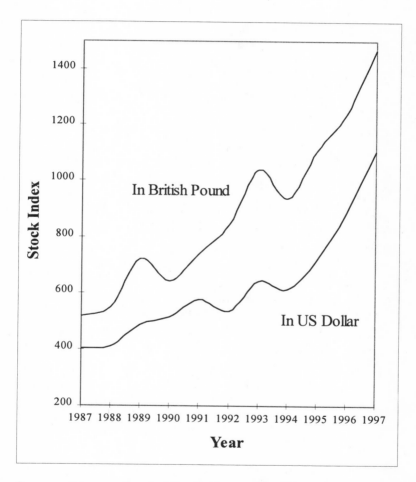

Source: Morgan Stanley Capital International and
MEI Indicators, OECD

have closely moved together. The United States is a global economic giant with its business empire spread far and wide. A speculative binge in America could not but spawn one in Europe, just as it did in the 1920s. In Italy, France, Sweden, Germany, the Netherlands and elsewhere, the share markets roared. From mid-1982 to the 1987 peak, Italian shares jumped 450 percent in terms of the US dollar, Swedish shares by 400 percent, Dutch stocks by 340 percent and Swiss stocks also by 400 percent.

The 1987 crash seems to have had a greater impact on western Europe than any other area. Since then European unemployment, for a variety of reasons, has been on the rise.

Britain seems to be the only nation that has escaped the trend. Overall, Europe's average unemployment rate was close to 12 percent, with Italy, France and Germany all near this average in 1997, while Spain suffered a lofty rate of 22 percent. One would think that high joblessness would keep stock markets on the leash. But only Italy has seen a subdued market, at least in terms of the dollar. In the go-go atmosphere since 1987, the US bubble seems to have infected every nation.

Even Spain, with a vast multitude of the unemployed, saw its share prices jump 82 percent in local currency terms. In France, the jump was over 220 percent between December 1987 to October 1997, measured in the dollar or the local currency; in Germany, it exceeded 225 percent, and in Britain it was more than 175 percent. While millions were without jobs, the speculators made mirth in western Europe.

Latin America

Latin America lives in the shadow of the US business empire, but the region's share market volatility is legendary. The stock price behavior in local currencies in Argentina and Brazil cannot even be graphed, because the return was beyond

Figure 9

Stock-Price Index In Argentina: 1987-96

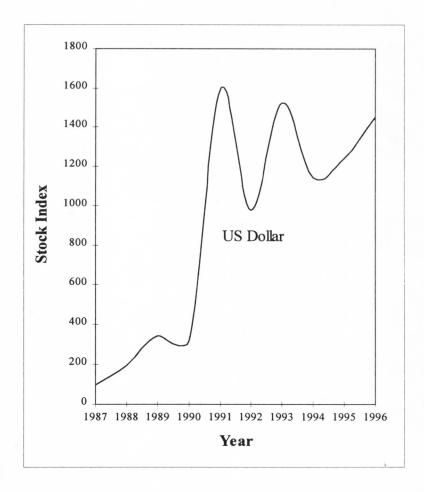

Source: Morgan Stanley Capital   International

127

Figure 10

Stock-Price Index In Brazil: 1987-96

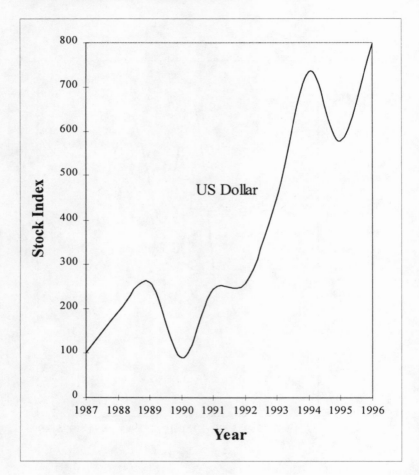

Source: Morgan Stanley Capital International

imagination. However, their inflation figures were also unimaginable, running into hundreds of percent per year. Needless to say, all this was a result of runaway government spending and extraordinary money growth.

Therefore, the only way you can make sense of their share markets is to study them in terms of the dollar. In this measure, the share price index in Argentina jumped from 100 in 1987 to·a peak of 1596 by the end of 1991, then crashed to 975 in 1992, climbing again to 1447 by the end of 1996. It was certainly an impressive performance, with the stock index soaring by 1347 percent in nine years.

The story of Brazil is much the same, with local currency stock returns unfathomable, but the return in terms of the dollar rising, with sharp ups and downs, by 698 percent from 1987 to 1996. The market performance here is somewhat subdued when compared to that in Argentina, but certainly worthy of a bubble.

Chile has had a more stable economy compared to both Brazil and Argentina. Chilean share markets enjoyed a steady but rousing improvement in terms of both local and foreign currencies till 1994. Thereafter the stock index fell but in 1996 was still far above the level in 1987. In nine years, the local currency stock yield was 1277 percent and in terms of the dollar the corresponding return was 654 percent.

Finally, we come to Mexico, which is a part of NAFTA (the North American Free Trade Agreement) and is now closely linked with the US economy. NAFTA came into effect in January 1994. Both American and Mexican experts argued that NAFTA would bring substantial benefits to both countries. Instead, the trade agreement was followed by a peso crisis, which shook the very foundations of the financial systems in the so-called emerging markets of the tiger economies and Latin America.

The Mexican currency crisis was the main reason for the

share price plunge in the emerging markets in 1994 and 1995. With Mexico's close proximity to its northern giant, its stock market is strongly affected by the New York Stock Exchange as well as the southward flow of US capital.

Measured in terms of the dollar, the Mexican stock index called the Bolsa jumped 1642 percent from 1987 to 1993--a clear case of a speculative bubble by anyone's definition. In 1994, however, the index crashed and plunged 44 percent in one year; next year, it fell by another 23 percent, as Mexico moved into a full-fledged depression. Factories closed, unemployment shot up and real wages tumbled, but American economists touted the gains the country had made under NAFTA.

President Clinton, alarmed that the peso crisis could spread to all emerging markets and finally to the United States, thus hurting his chances of reelection, quickly arranged for an aid package to bail out Mexico and to keep it from defaulting on its foreign debt. Mexico received $50 billion in loans from the United States and the International Monetary Fund.

The massive aid package stabilized the faltering southern economy, and share prices began to recover at the end of 1995. But so strong is the human need for quick money today, that the painful lessons of the Bolsa's crash were soon forgotten by speculators. In 1996, the dollar value of Mexican shares jumped 16 percent and another 30 percent by September 1997.

Other Countries

Among advanced economies, Denmark, Belgium and the Netherlands have also seen impressive gains in their share markets between 1987 and 1996. For instance, the Danish stock index jumped by 215 percent by 1996, the Belgian one by 138 percent, and the Dutch index by 228 percent, all in terms of their local currencies. By contrast, the gains made by Australia and Canada have been respectable but not up to the standards set by the United States. Canadian stocks rose only 82 percent and Australian ones 88 percent during this period. However, Eastern Europe has not suffered from the slow pace of stocks in recent years.

It is ironic as well as amusing that as soon as the satellite states were free from the Soviet dominance, their speculative activity took off. In Hungary, share prices soared 64% in terms of the dollar in just two years between 1994 and 1996; in Russia, with the economy in depression, the corresponding jump was 80%, whereas in Poland, the jump was 470% between 1992 to 1996. One would think that these countries were sizzling with mammoth rates of economic growth to generate such enormous returns on stock investment.

In reality, Eastern Europe was a hotbed of inflation, inefficiency, uncertainty and environmental pollution. In Russia, output actually fell sharply after the fall of communism, while unemployment soared.

Finally, let us consider the case of India, which, until 1992, was much more protectionist than it is today. With trade liberalization also came the inflow of foreign capital, and share prices rose impressively in 1993 and 1994; but political instability since then produced market losses, which were still not erased by the end of 1997.

An Overview

Let us now summarize our discussion thus far. Since the mid-1970s, many countries have experienced a big run-up in their share prices. It all started with Japan in 1975, where the stock market quickly came out of the global slump caused by the oil price shock of 1973. From 1982, other nations joined the speculative binge building up in Tokyo. Share markets crashed in October 1987, but recovered soon thereafter.

Thus, the global share mania continued, but was abruptly interrupted in 1990, when markets suffered heavy losses in Japan. This turned out to be a localized event, and share prices continued to climb in most areas of the world. Another blow to stocks came from the peso crisis toward the end of 1994, and several emerging markets began to slump.

However, the Dow and European stocks scarcely took notice. There were stock crashes in 1997 in Asia and Latin America, but not enough to cause a big jolt in the world's largest stock exchange located in New York. Thus, in spite of several stock market crashes in the 1990s, the global speculative bubble has not been punctured. It has been slowed somewhat, but the bullish stock sentiment, unleashed in the United States, Canada and Europe since 1982, still remains after 15 long years.

The Misinformation Economy

Many people have called the world economy since 1980 the information economy, where the international flow of ideas is vast and instantaneous. But it is more appropriate to term the global system a misinformation economy, simply because the views the public hears from experts and politicians are not objective but rooted in crass self-interest. When economists, crowned by the rich as distinguished professors and Nobel Prize winners, suggest that society should pass the tax burden from the wealthy to the rest to stimulate investment and growth, then clearly there is a problem right from the start.

This is a self-serving argument, which is reminiscent of the doctrine of the divine right of kings, who sought autocratic power in order to protect the people from anarchy. But who was going to protect the people from the kings? Similarly, who is going to save the poor from high taxation needed to finance government spending, when income tax rates are lowered for the wealthy?

In any case, when the top marginal income tax rate in America was over 80 percent, as in the 1950s and the 1960s, annual GDP growth averaged more than 4 percent. But when that tax rate was cut by more than half in the 1980s, the growth of output and investment fell sharply. Yet who knows this? All we hear is the misinformation that low income taxes, but not low Social Security and sales taxes that burden low-income groups, stimulate investment and growth.

Ours is a misinformation economy, and because of the pervasive influence of television and radio, the public is thoroughly convinced by the propaganda spewed by the hirelings of the affluent.

The global stock market bubbles discussed above are the product of the same misinformation. Let us first see what Wall Street brokers or their colleagues say in various countries. Their view is that high productivity growth resulting from new technology has led to a profit boom in the 1990s in many countries, resulting in a huge share price boom.

Another factor, according to them, is restrained inflation arising from increased globalization and international competition. This tends to decrease the rate of interest, making bonds less attractive and stocks more attractive. A lower interest rate also brings down business costs and further raises profits, which in turn lead to another stock market gain. This way share prices have been soaring time and time again.

In the view prevailing in the US and European stock exchanges, the fundamentals of low inflation, low interest rates and low unemployment in the United States are so good that stocks gain first in America and then elsewhere, because the American locomotive pulls the world's train.

However, Wall Street bankers and brokers have failed to

reveal that their much touted fundamentals have occurred many times in the past, but they did not produce a stock market of the millennium. Profits soared in the 1920s, while interest rates fell around the world. The Dow jumped from 72 at the end of 1920 to a peak of 360 by September 1929. This was a large gain of 400 percent, but nothing like the gain of over 900 percent in the 1980s and the 1990s.

There are some other reasons why the Dow along with several other share indexes continued to sizzle year after year in spite of the huge crash in 1987. The most important factor turns out to be the major growth in money and credit in two large economies, namely Japan and Germany.

Within the United States, the Fed under Chairman Alan Greenspan has kept a tight leash on credit. Money is needed to finance output expansion, in accordance with the law of supply and demand. Suppose the value of production rises by $100; then for the new supply to be sold, the consumers must have some more money to buy extra production. The supply of money comes from the notes printed by the Federal Reserve System or loans made by commercial banks.

There is a well-known law of economics that, since people's habits to use cash versus credit cards don't change for long (in technical language, velocity of money is constant), the growth of money equals the increase in the value of production, provided there is no speculation. If money growth exceeds the growth of monetary GDP, then the extra money is used to finance speculation in company shares, real estate and other assets.

In order to see if speculation is occurring in any country, we should compare its money growth with the growth of nominal GDP. Nominal GDP is the money value of production; it is the total value of output at current prices. A country calculates its output by first estimating nominal GDP and then adjusts it for any change in prices.

Let us take a look at the US economy between 1987 and

1996. The figure for money supply in various countries is provided by line 34 in an IMF publication called *International Financial Statistics*. The publication also contains data on nominal GDP. During the period in question, stock prices more than tripled, but US money growth was just 49 percent, while GDP growth was 68 percent.

Clearly, the American banking system was not responsible for the share mania. Then where did the money come from to finance the speculative bubble? From Japan and Germany, both of which had a large trade surplus with the United States. In Germany, money growth between 1987 and 1996 was 138 percent compared to nominal GDP growth of only 78 percent. The surplus money then financed not only the speculative mania inside the country but also in the United States.

In Japan, money supply shot up by 103 percent but GDP by only 44 percent in the same period. Clearly, a part of the extra money moved into US stock exchanges; another part went into the Tokyo exchange until it burst in 1990. After that the Japanese money moved feverishly into America and many other countries, thereby fueling asset inflation.

Normally, when a bubble economy punctures and a recession follows, money supply falls sharply. That is exactly what happened around the world in the early 1930s. But this time, thanks to global financial deregulation inspired by US experts, Japan's money supply actually shot up in the 1990s.

Soon after the stock market crash of 1990, money growth was exceptionally low at about 2 percent per year. But then the Bank of Japan brought interest rates down to their lowest level in history to reduce the cost of deposits for faltering banks, and a monetary explosion followed. Individuals borrowed money and invested it in stock markets around the world. Japanese banks also lent nearly free money (deposit interest of 1 percent is close to zero) to individuals and financial institutions in the United States and East Asia, thereby inflating the global bubble. Such practices were banned prior to 1975.

Thanks to surplus money from Germany and Japan, the whole world is now a bubble economy. Even Japan, where the local bubble burst in 1990, is still a part of the global bubble, because its governments failed to take any serious action. They continued their old policies of export promotion by keeping the yen low relative to the dollar, mark and the pound.

In the 1980s, Japan's banks made bad loans to land speculators at home; in the 1990s, they have made bad loans to speculators in the economies of Asian tigers. So the bubble continues in Japan.

Toward the end of 1997, four prominent financial institutions failed, namely Hokkaido Takushoku Bank, Nissan Life Insurance Company, Sanyo Securities, and Yamaichi Securities. The closing of Yamaichi was the biggest industrial failure in Japan since the Second World War. Something previously unthinkable and politically unpermissible was happening in 1997, seven years after the bursting of the bubble.

In other countries also, where stock markets have sizzled, money growth has been exceptionally high. In Europe, Denmark, the Netherlands, Norway and Finland have seen high rates of monetary expansion, whereas other advanced economies such as Australia and Canada have also done the same.

Among the Asian baby tigers, all have experienced money growth rates far in excess of nominal GDP growth, whereas Latin America exercised no monetary discipline whatsoever. Apart from Argentina and Brazil, both of which suffered hyper-money expansion and inflation, Chile and Mexico also saw an exceptional boom in credit. Stock exchanges in emerging markets were thus lubricated not only by German and Japanese money but also by their own credit growth.

The Dow Jones Index or the Dow was first calculated in

1885. In November 1982, it crossed the one thousand mark. The Dow took almost a century to get past 1,000; but in the next 15 years, it rocketed past 8,000. Have the natural laws of supply and demand changed suddenly? No. But the nature of the world economy has.

Through financial deregulation inspired by American brokers and bankers, itching to make quick and vast amounts of money, there has been an unprecedented explosion of money and credit around the planet. This, not the so-called fundamentals, has generated the global bubbles in which many countries are now trapped. Multi-millionaires in America wanted to become billionaires, and they did not care if they sank the world's boat in the process. Even the more recent savings and loan crisis of the mid-1990s, caused by financial deregulation did not faze them.

America went on a spree of financial deregulation after Ronald Reagan became president in 1981. Interest rates were no longer set by the government. Banks were permitted to pay interest on checking accounts, a practice that was outlawed in the mid-1930s. As a result of these and other measures, much fraud occurred in the savings and loan industry. Many such companies went bankrupt, and the taxpayer was saddled with the bill that came due, because the deposits of defunct corporations were insured by the government. All in all, the country paid a hefty price of $200 billion for its misadventure in financial deregulation.

The acolytes of such deregulation forgot the precious lessons of the 1930s and more recently of the 1980s out of blind greed. They continued to paddle their self interest as sound economic policy, and now the global economy stands perilously on the brink of a precipice, ready to collapse any moment. A few more waves of the 1930s style competitive devaluations, and the world economic order will go to pieces.

Of course, avarice is nothing new. It is as old as humanity itself; but the government policy should not promote greed, because the end result is nothing short of a calamity. This is what the state did in the 1920s, and then again in the 1980s and the 1990s. I hope the aftermath is different this time.

* * *

5. Stock Market Crashes of 1997

Toward the end of 1997, as I watched the money shows on CNN and CNBC, I frequently heard a term called "competitive devaluations." The term caught my attention, because until then it had been used by economists to describe the international currency turmoil of the late 1920s and the 1930s. High foreign debt and trade deficits make a deadly combination that in the past has brought many economies down to their knees. As a recent case, this happened to Mexico in 1994-1995, when the country sank into a depression, which still afflicts the poor.

During the late 1920s, the world wheat market was under great pressure because of oversupply that lead to a sharp fall in the product's price. Argentina, a major borrower of foreign money and a wheat exporter, was thus forced to devalue its currency in 1928. Its neighbor, Uruguay, then did the same in 1929. Other wheat exporters were Australia and New Zealand. They were thousands of miles away, but that did not keep them from depreciating their own currencies in 1929.

The world was not the global village then that it is today. It took a year before Argentina's devaluation had any effect on its neighbor and other wheat exporters. Today, we essentially live in an inter-linked world, where information travels fast, and the economy is globalized. Competitive devaluations move swiftly across nations.

Devaluations of Baby Tigers

Thailand is one of the ringleaders among the baby tigers. It has had a high and steady growth rate approximating 8 percent since 1955. In 1989, it had a small foreign debt totaling $12 billion. Its neighbor, Malaysia, was in the same position-- prosperous and relatively debt free. Its foreign liabilities were a paltry $14 billion. Thanks to globalization and financial deregulation that accelerated the international flow of speculative capital, both countries ended up with a heavy debt load by the end of 1997--$50 billion for Malaysia and a hefty $95 billion for Thailand.

All the baby tigers were now burdened with overseas debt. This, along with their heavy import surpluses, made them vulnerable to currency speculators.

High growth rates and liberalized financial markets have endeared the cub economies to foreign investors and speculators since 1993. European and US mutual funds have been pouring billions of dollars into the stocks of emerging markets. Investment advisers have fervently preached the gospel of global diversification in recent years. In addition, Japanese banks lent money at low interest rates, which in turn fueled property speculation. Thus a speculative binge developed in the cubs of Asia in both shares and real estate.

In 1996, Thailand had a trade deficit of $14.5 billion.

In order to attract overseas investment, Thailand had kept its currency stable at the rate of about 25 bahts per dollar. But as the trade shortfall mounted in 1997, it was increasingly clear that the link could no longer be maintained at the old level. Currency speculators began selling the baht in foreign exchange markets; foreign capital began to flee, and the value of the baht fell sharply in July.

This was a shock to overseas investors, who were caught off guard, even though similar events had occurred just two years ago in Mexico. But the country had been bailed out and foreign investors had been protected by an aid package arranged by the United States and the International Monetary Fund. Investors had expected the same type of aid for Thailand; here aid did come, but only after the crisis came to the surface. The IMF arranged a quick loan of $17 billion in exchange for austerity measures to be adopted by the government of Thailand.

As in the case of Mexico in 1995, the austerity program included a rise in taxes, a cut in the government budget deficit and a reduction in money growth. However, because of the shaky political situation, the Thai government could not adopt the program and the baht continued to sink.

Currency depreciations normally have a tendency to spread among nations competing for similar products. But they take some time. This time, however, Thai devaluation spread quickly among the baby tigers, because they were in the same boat of high debt coupled with trade deficits. Foreign money fled overnight from stock exchanges. East Asian currencies fell like dominoes. First Thailand, then Malaysia, followed by Indonesia and the Philippines felt the jolt of devaluations. As *Time* magazine put it in its November 3rd issue:

> On July 2 the baht plunged more than 12% in value against the greenback. Then it crashed into the Philippines, Malaysia and Indonesia, where government officials were forced to devalue their currencies. That triggered a region-wide crisis, in which stock markets gave up as much as 35% of their value, inflated real estate prices fell through the floor, banks collapsed, and hundreds of thousands of Southeast Asians, rich and poor, lost their jobs and fortunes (p. 44).

It is interesting   that experts saw the same sound fundamentals in the baby tigers as they do in the United States, which also, after all, has a hefty foreign debt and a trade deficit. On the same page, *Time* quotes a World Bank official as saying, "There were no obvious warning signals of the kind of catastrophe that was about to hit Indonesia." Growth was high, inflation was low and exports were projected to soar. In a way, the United States is just a giant version of Thailand. Both have had high growth, low unemployment, but a giant foreign debt and trade deficit.

International efforts to contain the currency tremors proved abortive. Wall Street brokers shrugged off the Asian crisis. They felt that the cubs were too small to have a significant effect on a far-away giant like the United States. The nearby Japan, however, felt the tremors immediately. As much as 44 percent of its exports go to tiger economies. Vanishing foreign investment and lending meant a major slowdown in the lands of baby tigers; Japan was bound to contract further. Therefore, the Nikkei came under pressure immediately, while the Dow was unaffected.

142

Devaluations of Little Tigers

American brokers and experts thought, at least hoped, that the currency crisis would be limited to the baby tigers, and others, such as the much larger little tigers, would be able to withstand the assault of speculators. Their understanding and hope proved mistaken. In July, the baby tigers were invaded by speculators. In August came the turn of Hong Kong, Taiwan and Singapore, none of which had any foreign debt and enjoyed an export surplus.

History shows that sooner or later even seemingly strong economies succumb to the stress of competitive de-valuations. Singapore's dollar quickly gave in; so did its stock market. Taiwan followed suit. But Hong Kong successfully fought the assault.

Hong Kong had been taken over by China on July 1st. China, with its vast dollar reserve, was not prepared to let its newly acquired territory suffer a currency setback without a fight. Besides, Hong Kong had a dollar hoard of its own worth $88 billion. The currency speculators could not bring the Hong Kong dollar down, but the territory paid a heavy price. In order to add luster to its currency, Hong Kong authorities raised their interest rates and attracted more foreign money, but the stock market crashed in the process.

September was relatively quiet, as both American and Japanese governments were busy arranging aid packages--$17 billion for Thailand, $23 billion for Indonesia. Then came October, a month notorious for some of the biggest stock market meltdowns in history. Remember Black Monday on October 19, 1987, or the Black days in October 1929. Thus anxiety was already running high that month in 1997. Then

143

came the stunning news of another crash in Hong Kong on October 23rd, combined with heavy losses in the Tokyo exchange.

With cheaper currencies in its backyard, Hong Kong became an awfully expensive place to live. Tourism, one of the main industries, plunged. Speculators took another shot at the currency, and Hong Kong raised its interest rates again. The last week of October witnessed a share market carnage around the planet.

A 10 percent crash in Hong Kong on October 23rd and another 6 percent four days later sent shivers around the globe. The same day, on October 27th, the Dow Jones Index, so far immune to all that noise in Asia, fell 554 points, which was the largest point drop in Wall Street history. In percentage terms, the fall was only 7 percent, but the investing world had been shaken.

No longer were the fundamentals, of which the financial analysts constantly bragged, so sound; something was wrong, but why would any broker or politician admit that there was a problem? Instead, the experts chanted the same mantra: the US economy has low inflation, unemployment and interest rates; so everything is OK; don't worry; don't panic. Later, on November 13th, Alan Greenspan actually suggested that the Asian market crashes could even benefit the United States by suppressing inflation. "The basics of the US economy are strong," were the soothing words of Cathy Minehan, president of the Boston Federal Reserve Bank" (*Time*, November 10, 1997, p. 39).

November saw the currency crisis spread to Korea, which has an economy twice the size of Thailand. Korea has an even bigger debt and foreign trade problems. Its corporations have a lot of short-term debt, some $60 to $70 billion, that will come

144

due at the end of 1997; but its foreign exchange reserves are less than $30 billion, not enough to fight a speculative assault in its currency. Like Thailand, Malaysia and Indonesia, hundreds of Korean companies have declared bankruptcy and laid off workers. In December, the IMF offered an aid package worth $60 billion to Korea.

The Tokyo stock exchange continued its decline even after the Dow stabilized. On November 14th, the Nikkei hit a low of 15,082, down about 25 percent for the year. Korea's large companies were swamped with unpaid loans. Five of the 30 largest enterprises had suffered heavy losses. In late November, the country abandoned its efforts to defend the won because of heavy foreign exchange losses. The speculators lost a battle in Hong Kong, but won a big victory at the Korean battle ground.

Latin America

After a prolonged spell of nervousness and depression, Mexico had recovered somewhat by the summer of 1997. The Bolsa stock index had jumped 40 percent that year, and the peso had stabilized at 7.7 pesos to the dollar. Its southern neighbors in Latin America had once again reverted to the precious task of stock and property speculation. Their cozy world was also shaken by the currency crisis that began in Thailand.

Mexico suffered another Black Monday on October 27th. The Bolsa's main index plunged 13 percent; so did the stock index in Brazil and Argentina. Venezuela's index dropped 9 percent. For the last week in October, stocks fell by over 30 percent in Latin America and Mexico--a mini-crash compared to the Asian debacle.

Interest rates rose in all the emerging markets. In Brazil,

145

they were as high as 45 percent. By the end of 1997, auto sales had shrunk in East Asia as well as Latin America; thousands of businesses had closed. The currency crisis was taking an ugly turn with bad consequences for many economies. By November's end, as reported by the *Wall Street Journal*, share prices in the baby tigers had plummeted more than 40 percent for the year, with Thailand taking a hit of as much as 50 percent. Among the little tigers the carnage was not quite as bad, with Korea and Singapore being the worst hit at 35 percent. Clearly, share markets in Asia and Latin America had crashed in 1997.

Relishing the sweet taste of success in East Asia, currency speculators turned their sights on Brazil, another economy with a huge debt and trade balance problems. Brazilian authorities took immediate steps to protect their currency, the real. They spent $11 billion to buy their own currency and doubled the interest rate. The real came under intense selling pressure, but it withstood the assault. The currency did not lose value, and the speculators suffered losses.

Brazil's successful defense of the real helped Argentina, which would have to match any currency depreciation by its northern neighbor. Argentina sends 30 percent of its exports to Brazil, and when the real remained stable, the Argentineans breathed a sigh of relief. However, high Brazilian interest rates, if continued, would mean a slowdown for the entire southern continent. There was also talk of an austerity program to lower Brazil's budget deficit through a rise in the income tax rate. All this signals a slowdown.

Other Countries

Western Europe's response to the Asian contagion was the

146

same as that of the United States. The continent was disturbed by the final week's events in October, but it chanted the same old mantra of sound fundamentals, and went back to business as usual. The region's market decline from the peak reached in August was about 10 percent, the same as in America. Share prices in Canada and Australia behaved in much the same way. However, Eastern Europe was shaken by the jolt from Asia. The Skate index of 50 stocks in Russia, for instance, fell 30% below its August peak.

The Fundamental Problem

So far the US experts, along with the IMF, the World Bank and Japanese officials, have not been able to contain the currency crisis. They have promised aid packages, accepted the currency devaluations of many of the tigers and repeatedly assured international investors of the strength of the world economy. But the crisis continues to spread, with Korea, and Japan itself, being the countries under close scrutiny by US experts. More dominoes are going to fall and soon. The reason is that the so-called sound fundamentals of Wall Streeters have created a serious global imbalance.

The fundamental economic force underlying any economy is the force of supply and demand. All other factors work through this mechanism. Therefore, in order to examine the soundness of an economic system, we should examine if demand and supply are in balance. If not, the system is bound to fall apart sooner or later.

Supply springs from production or labor productivity, and demand from wages. If wages rise in proportion to productivity, then both supply and demand grow equally and their balance is maintained over time. But if wages move slower or faster than productivity, then the balance may be artificially preserved in the short run by some other factors, but in the long run there is trouble either in the form of inflation or recession and depression. When demand grows faster than supply, prices rise and inflation results. In the opposite case when wages lag behind productivity and demand rises slower than supply, inflation falls and unemployment moves up, as businesses are stuck with unsold goods, that cause layoffs.

In both Japan and the United States wages grew slower than productivity in the 1980s and the 1990s, but in Japan the problem began in the mid-1970s. We have already seen this in Chapter 3.

In the United States, trouble began brewing in the early 1980s after a steep recession ended in 1982. Because of the recession and increasing globalization, the real wage, which is the purchasing power of one's salary, began to fall for the vast majority of workers. This fact is well documented in the *Economic Report of the President* and many well known books. In fact, until 1989 only real wages fell, while real income in two-earner families kept rising; but, following the recession of 1990, even real family income began to fall. All this time productivity continued to rise, and a gap began to develop between supply and demand.

Rising population itself generated an increase in demand, but, because of stagnant wages, demand growth lagged behind the output growth arising from rising productivity. Another factor limiting demand growth was the transfer of the tax burden from the rich to the poor. Income tax rates paid mostly by the rich fell after 1981, while Social Security taxes, borne mostly by the poor and the middle class, soared. Since the wealthy spend a smaller proportion of after-tax income than the poor, the transfer of the tax burden further restrained the growth in demand.

For a while, the supply-demand gap can be plugged by other factors. For instance, in Japan, the gap was eliminated by exporting the increased supply. The problem was postponed until 1990, when the stock market crashed, domestic demand fell, and the United States resisted a further rise in trade deficits with Japan. In the United States, the supply-demand gap was eliminated by bank loans and consumer debt, which artificially lift consumer demand. Cheaper bank loans stimulated housing and business spending on investment. Investment spending raises demand in the short run but increases supply in the long run.

As the supply-demand gap was eliminated, profits rose sharply, because productivity soared while wage costs fell. Corporate downsizing, whereby companies replaced high-paid workers with low-paid ones, also kept a lid on labor costs. Thus, profits soared, and so did stock prices. And with all that money coming from Germany and Japan, the stock market rise turned into a speculative bubble.

A similar process occurred around the world. Wages lagged behind productivity, but bank lending to consumers and businesses filled the brewing demand-supply gap. There also profits rocketed, along with share markets.

The growth process tinged with speculation may carry on uninterrupted for a decade or as long as 15 or 16 years. In the 1920s, the process could last no more than a decade. In Japan, it went on for 15 years, before coming to an abrupt halt. Seldom in history has it been extended past a decade and a half.

The current worldwide speculative binge began in the middle of 1982. It continued, with brief interruptions, until mid-1997, when the Thai currency debacle brought it to a

149

close. Now the markets are crashing, speculation is unraveling and a period of reckoning has begun.

The speculative growth process ends when banks slow their lending or debt-burdened consumers reduce their borrowing. The artificial props for demand vanish and the supply-demand gap, hidden for a while, comes to the surface. If the potential gap is hidden for a short period, only a short-lived recession then develops. However, if it lasts a decade or more, stock markets crash and a depression follows. In fact, the longer and deeper the gap, the longer and deeper the ensuing pain and depression.

Once again, for emphasis: Productivity is the source of supply, wages are the source of demand. If the gap between the two grows, as in the 1920s, stock markets first sky-rocket, then crash. Crashes occurred in 1929 in America, in Japan in the 1990s, and now in Japan, South East Asia and Latin America in 1997.

In the case of the US economy today, there is another complication. Inside America, there is no excess supply. In fact, US national demand exceeds the supply and the difference is the trade deficit. The supply-demand imbalance exists in the world economy, though, as multinational companies have built hundreds of new factories in the tiger economies, India, Latin America, Mexico, China and Eastern Europe. Most manufacturing industries suffer from overcapacity. Autos, computers, machine tools, consumer electronics, appliances, all have excessive productive capacity, but it exists outside American borders.

The speculative growth process is disrupted at a critical point, when banks wake up and discover that they have made too many risky loans, which may not be paid back. That is when they trim their lending. The critical point arrived in

150

South East Asia in mid-1997, when speculators assaulted the debt-ridden Thai currency. Suddenly, Thai banks discovered their folly of reckless lending for office projects that stood empty, shopping malls that were unoccupied, and so on. The currency devaluation sent a wake-up call and loans fell sharply. Now consumer demand has fallen to the level supported by low wages, and productive capacity or supply far exceeds demand. This was Japan's problem after 1990; now the entire Asian economy is Japanized, especially if you count the enormous new capacity that has been built in China in recent years.

Some people believe that China could be another Korea, where thousands of workers have been laid of in recent months. Reporter Seth Faison, writing in *New York Times*, November 27, 1997, argues that "If one country looks vulnerable to the kind of financial disaster now engulfing much of Asia, it is China." Since 1994, Chinese currency, the yuan, has appreciated 25% relative to the US dollar, while the currencies of the neighboring tigers have mostly depreciated. This is likely to hinder Chinese exports and add to Beijing's financial troubles.

Foreign investment in China fell 40% in 1997, and this could create foreign debt woes in the long run. Fortunately, the country has little short-term debt and has not attracted much overseas capital into its stock markets, so that there is little danger from sudden capital flight. Nevertheless, if China were forced to devalue the yuan, it could set off another round of devaluations and currency instability in Asia.

In spite of an overvalued currency, China's exceptionally low wages could put even more pressure on the tiger economies and their wages, which could fall. Falling wages will exacerbate the supply-demand imbalance, which has now become visible, so much so that stock markets in the baby tigers have crashed by more than 40 percent in less than six months. The speed of this crash is faster than that of America in 1929 and that of Japan in 1990. All this suggests that immediate prospects in Asia are gloomy, and we must take urgent action to avoid the type of calamity that struck the world in the 1930s.

* * *

6. The Future

The speculative bubble burst open in Japan in 1990, but it continued to expand in the United States and most other countries, and turned into a global bubble. Even though stock markets in Asia and Latin America crashed at the end of 1997, the bubble was not yet pierced; it had been deflated somewhat, but not punctured. This is because the United States, the world's locomotive and the largest economy, experienced only a slight decline in its share markets. The Dow hovered around 7,800, which was below its August peak but still more than nine times its low point in 1982.

Western Europe, Canada and Australia also suffered only minor drops in share prices. Thus the global bubble continued to flourish as 1997 came to a close. Although Japan had already suffered a seven-year long stagnation, it was still a part of the international bubble economy, which it had helped to build through its trade surpluses and reckless lending to Korea and the baby tigers.

The global bubble had localized balloons in various nations, with the US balloon still the largest in the world. Europe's bubble was next in size. Japan's balloon was small relative to

153

what it had been at the end of 1989, but it was still filled with hot speculative air. Japan's banks were saddled with numerous bad loans, domestic as well as foreign, although share and land prices had indeed collapsed.

The Global Bubble Economy

It is a great irony that Japan, which had a bubble economy in the 1980s and whose bubble burst in 1990, now finds itself an integral part of the global bubble economy. The country has been in a slump for seven long years, and its asset markets no longer sizzle, but now it is even more dependent on the health of foreign markets, which have bubble economies of their own. Japanese industry faces as much danger in 1998 as it did in 1990. This it seems is the price to be paid from government inaction. It is reminiscent of the US government's indifference in the early 1930s, when bank after bank collapsed, but the Fed took no preventive measure.

History tells us that bubble economies normally last seven years before bursting. Sometime, as in the 1920s, they live through the entire decade, and at rare moments in history, they have lasted as long as 16 years. Mexico's localized bubble, for instance, began to build in 1988 and crashed in 1995; the same thing happened in Chile. Thailand's local bubble started to inflate in 1987 and then burst in 1994. Thus, speculative manias often collapse in their 7th or 8th years.

Once in a while, when a socio-economic system or a way of life is about to be transformed, bubbles live as long as 15 or 16 years. The Japanese local bubble started in 1975 and then split open in 1990 and 1991. The current global bubble, built around the US financial markets, started in 1982 and has lasted till 1997. Its 16th anniversary will be in June or August 1998, depending on how you pick its starting point. If nature continues to follow its laws of history, the current global bubble will burst by August 1998.

Nature's rules cannot be defied forever. Individuals and nations may believe that they can violate the laws that nature has upheld for centuries; but in the end, they are shocked and suffer losses. It is not possible to fool mother nature for long. The crowd of speculators that used to chant, "Japan is different," now thinks differently. Similarly, the US experts who frequently cite their misleading fundamentals to keep the public buying their company's shares, will also see the light sometime soon.

Suppose my calculations are off by six months. Then the bubble could last through 1998 and burst in early 1999. But burst it will. I have no doubt about that.

The European Bubble

In any case, the US bubble will be the last to burst; this is because America is at the center of its business empire and other nations are at the periphery. When an empire disintegrates, the center is the last to fall. The outermost territories go down first, then those in the neighborhood, and finally the center. When Soviet communism fell in the 1990s, East Germany was the first to disintegrate after the fall of the Berlin Wall in November 1989. Then came the turn of communism in Poland, Romania, Hungary, Czechoslovakia and Yugoslavia. These were the distant satellites of the Soviet Union. First they fell; then nearby provinces such as the Ukraine, Armenia, Georgia, Azerbaijan among others declared independence. Finally, communism fell in Russia which was at the center of the Soviet empire.

155

In the forthcoming demise of the US business empire, American markets, being at the center, will thus be the last to fall. In the 1990s, the stock market crashes have been recurring in the peripheries but not in America, Europe, Canada, and Australia. Japan suffered devastating blows in 1990 and 1991. Markets also crashed in Taiwan, Thailand, Singapore and Mexico between 1993 and 1995, and then again in 1997.

When the peripheries are hurt, the center also feels the pain but not to the same extent. Likewise, the US share markets do react negatively to turmoil in outer regions, but then recover quickly.

Trouble is fast approaching the United States. In 1990, Japan's share prices crashed; in 1997, seven years later, Japan, the tigers, Eastern Europe and Latin America suffered. In the next crash, it could be Asia, Latin America, Europe and possibly Australia and Canada. The United States will indeed feel the pain, but will brush it aside.

Its markets will fall, but then quickly recover a part of the loss just as they did in August, October and November of 1997. But each percentage decline is likely to be worse than the previous decline.

For instance, on one August day in 1997, the Dow fell about 250 points and then quickly recovered; but the next time around in October, it fell 554 points, and only partially recovered the loss. In 1998, there will be a series of crashes around the world, but at first they will be worse in outer territories than in the United States. The supply-demand gap is extraordinarily large in the world today, and until this gap disappears, share prices will remain under pressure.

Every crash will be worse than the previous crash. In every share market, there are some bulls and some bears. In the lingo of stock exchanges, the bulls expect share prices to rise, whereas the bears expect them to fall. Share markets, therefore, are frequent battle grounds for bulls and bears. When the optimists have an upper hand, stocks gain; when pessimists win, stocks lose. In Japan, bears have been winning the battle since 1990, although they consistently lost ground between 1975 and 1989.

The bulls have been victorious in US markets for a long time. In fact, most wealthy investors are optimists nowadays. The share price crashes in 1998 are likely to occur around long holidays and during vacations, when the bulls are away, relaxing at beaches or making merry in tourist towns. When the bulls are not at home to defend their turf, bears will triumph.

The day after the October meltdown in New York, when the Dow fell 554 points, IBM and other cash rich companies made loud announcements to buy their own shares. This is how the bulls fought back after the bears had shaken the markets the day before. During vacations, however, many investors leave town. They are not around to respond quickly to sudden crises.

Furthermore, the volume of stock trading also then declines so that share price movements are magnified. On a low trading day, a slight case of bad news can cause nervous selling and a gloomy sentiment, which, when continued over a few days, culminates in a market crash. And bad news will be abundant in the near future. Furthermore, 1998 will also be the 16th year of the current global bubble that began in the United States. I know of no speculative mania in history that lived past its 16th birthday.

The Chinese New Year normally comes at the beginning of February. Many Chinese investors in Hong Kong, Taiwan and Singapore will then be away to celebrate the New Year. That is when we should expect another crash to strike Asia, Latin

157

America and possibly Europe, with America taking a hit but shrugging it aside.

Spring break occurs in the United States in the middle of March. If February escapes a crash, then March is likely to get it next, or both months could see market meltdowns.

The real battle between the bulls and bears will come in the summer of 1998. A lot of people then take a break from work and the business of investing. Summer begins in June and ends in September. There will be a lot of crashes in these months. October is traditionally a period of market pessimism. The bearish sentiment could be especially dominant in this month.

The next period to watch would be the end of 1998, around Christmas and the New Year. My month-by-month forecasts, of course, could be off by a few days. But, what is certain is that 1998 will see a series of stock market crashes around the world, including the United States.

It is the nature of market crashes that the share index tends to move back to the starting point. After stocks crashed in New York in 1929, the Dow fell more than 80 percent in three years. In Japan, the Nikkei index fell 60 percent between 1990 and 1993. History thus gives us some clues about the likely fall of the Dow, the Nikkei and other stock indexex in 1998 and beyond.

If the Dow declines less than 50 percent in 1998, then it will continue to crash in 1999, following the same quarterly pattern as in the previous year. All in all, it could tumble as much as 80 percent, the same level as in the early 1930s. For the Nikkei to decline 80 percent below its peak of around 39,000 reached in 1989, the index will have to plunge to 7,800. In other words, the Nikkei could also fall sharply in 1998 and 1999 from its value of about 16,000 at the end of 1997.

The Unfolding Scenario

How will the Asian crisis reach the shores of America and Europe? The currencies of the Asian tigers and Japan have declined sharply in recent months. Their exports have become cheaper abroad and imports have become expensive at home. They have also seen business closures and layoffs. Asian consumers have been cutting back on their household spending. Expensive foreign goods and falling demand will sharply trim imports; but lower prices will stimulate exports. Thus, in the months to come, Europe and the United States will see a sharp increase in their trade deficits with Asia.

Companies in Europe and North America will suffer sales losses; their profits will fall, and that means crushing losses in share prices, which have been soaring from the promise of ever-increasing corporate profits.

At first, shareholders in Europe and North America will be complacent; they will be advised by Wall Street brokers and bankers not to panic, because the US fundamentals are supposedly very sound. Bill Clinton and Alan Greenspan will reassure the public and possibly lower the interest rates. The experts will sing the glories of long-term investing to the public. As a result, after each downturn, stock markets will recover somewhat.

But the global supply-demand gap will not disappear, and we will continue to see crashes in the financial markets. At some point the public or institutional investors will panic. That is when a thunderbolt will strike the New York Stock Exchange, perhaps in the summer of 1998, or around Christmas, and definitely by the end of 1999.

The thunderbolt could come in one massive jolt or, as with Japan in 1990, in a series of weekly market declines.

159

America, after all, is a giant version of Thailand. As with the Baby Tiger, the United States has a mountain of foreign debt coupled with a vast trade deficit. The US economy and share markets have prospered from hefty capital inflows from abroad. The internal debt in America is also high. The US economy will collapse just as fast as the Thai economy. Nature is not partial to any nation or people. When natural laws are violated for so long, the end result is a Shakespearean tragedy.

First the peripheries fall, and then the center. When the center disintegrates, the outer areas suffer some more. The thunderbolt in New York will then send shock waves around the world. Stocks will crash, once again, from Tokyo to London to Toronto to Sydney.

The Fall of the Business Empire

Like any other empire, the American business empire will also fall. The question is not if, but when.

A close look at any society reveals that there are three possible sources of political power--military, intellect and money. Religion may also yield social influence, but priests dominate society through their mastery of scriptures and rituals. In other words, they also utilize their intellect to control and influence people. Thus, there are only three sources of political leadership. As a result, through the pages of history we find that society is sometime dominated by warriors, sometime by intellectuals (including priests) and sometime by the wealthy.

What is more interesting is that the age of the military, in which the army rules, is followed by the age of intellectuals, wherein the educated bureaucracy reigns, and then by the age of the affluent or acquisitors, in which money rules. Eventually, the acquisitors acquire so much wealth that other groups of people have to spend most of their time at work just to earn a living. That is when people get fed up with the rich, and overthrow the rule of money and the institutions associated with it. After that warriors dominate society again and the cycle of social evolution begins anew. In other words warriors come back to power, followed by intellectuals and acquisitors and so on.

This is the law of social cycles authored by my late teacher, P.R. Sarkar. For instance, the Western world and Japan have passed through two such cycles since the birth of Christ. In Western society, the Roman empire was an age of warriors, the rule of the Catholic Church was an age of intellectuals, and feudalism was an age of the wealthy. This completed one rotation of the social cycle.

Another rotation began when feudalism was replaced by the dominance of army generals who founded kingdoms and dynasties; this was followed by the rule of prime ministers and diplomats, or another age of intellectuals. Today, and since about 1860, the capitalistic West is in another age of acquisitors. The prominent role of the American business empire suggests that much of the world today is in the era of the wealthy.

In 1978, I wrote a book entitled *The Downfall of Capitalism and Communism,* in which I explained the law of social cycles and predicted that both capitalism and Soviet communism would collapse by the year 2000. My reasoning was that Russia and its satellites would move from the age of warriors to the era of intellectuals, whereas the West would move into another age of warriors. The future era of the military would be one where army officers are democratically elected as top political leaders without any help from the wealthy.

At the end of the era of acquisitors, there is extreme debt and poverty, because the rich elites have acquired much of the nation's wealth. That is the point where feudalism met its death knell and that is where we stand today. Just one percent of Americans own more than 40 percent of wealth. Half of all Americans have less than a thousand dollars in the bank. Consumer debt is at record high.

The acquisitive era or capitalism is about to end, the same way Soviet communism collapsed right before your eyes. And the beginning of the end will start in 1999, soon after the thunderbolt strikes the New York stock market.

The US business empire seems to be following the same pattern that the Roman empire followed in its final years. Rome had colonized many nearby and distant territories, extracting taxes from them to finance its trade deficit. Later, warriors from these very territories began invading the empire. First, the peripheries fell, then the nearby provinces, and finally the capital itself.

The US business empire is now being invaded by businessmen in the peripheries. They have already captured many markets inside the United States. The country no longer produces certain products that it invented and pioneered. Television, VCR, consumer electronics, textiles, ship-building, etc., are some of the US industries that have practically vanished under the fierce assault of imports.

A vaster flood of imports, bolstered by Asian devaluations, is about to inundate the remaining American industries. By itself, the flood would not cause enough damage to bring down the system. True, the living standard or real wages would fall some more, but the system would survive. However, America is in the midst of the fattest speculative

162

bubble in history; it is also, as stated earlier, the world's biggest debtor with a giant trade deficit, a deadly combination that has already devastated some Asian tigers.

Eventually, the import invasion would do to the American business empire what the so-called barbarian invasions did to the Roman empire. After the demise of Rome's domains, a new era was born. The same pattern will unfold in the West, starting at the end of 1999.

Interest Rates

How would interest rates behave in 1998? With each stock market crash, interest rates could actually fall in America. In Japan, they cannot fall any further, having bottomed out already. Investors today are exposed to great risk around the globe. Once they are bitten by tumbling share prices, they will rush into relatively risk-free securities such as US government bonds. When the peripheries begin to fall, people run to the center for shelter. Similarly, investors will rush into American government bonds, bringing US interest rates down.

Interest rates could also fall in Europe, especially in Britain, France and Germany. Even the debt-ridden Italy could see a decline in bond yields, but they will rise in the third world and, at least initially, in the economies of Asian tigers.

These will just be the immediate effects of stock market crashes. Once the New York exchange suffers a meltdown, capital will flow out of the United States. US interest rates could then rise.

The Dollar

In 1995, the US dollar simply collapsed, hitting a low of 80 yen and 1.3 Deutche marks in April. Since then the Greenback has been slowly recovering. At the end of 1997, the dollar was very strong compared to its level in recent years. The dollar rose relative to the German mark, the yen, the Italian lira, the won, and the currencies of baby tigers.

Until the Dow itself suffers a stunning and lasting crash, the dollar could gain further as other stock exchanges continue to face huge losses. But after the collapse of the Dow, the dollar will fall and could test the lows reached in the first half of 1995. Other international currencies will gain relative to the dollar. The yen and the Deutche mark will perhaps be major beneficiaries.

Gold

Gold prices plunged in 1997. They could stay low for much of 1998, and recover only after the fall of the US dollar. People turn to the yellow metal when prices rise fast or when chaos prevails in society. Gold is a good hedge against inflation, uncertainty and calamity. Inflation is low in America, Japan and Germany today, the three largest economies in the world. There is no inflationary push to gold prices now, and the precious metal plunged in value in 1997.

Share price crashes will cripple consumer confidence, lower demand and inflation. Therefore, gold could lose more of its luster. Only after investors see a major fall in the value of the dollar will gold recover. Just how strong this recovery will be is hard to determine in advance. In the event there is political chaos along with economic woes, gold prices will soar.

* * *

Deflation versus Inflation

In the United states, Fed Chairman Alan Greenspan, along with the financial markets, has been constantly worried about the onset of inflation. In fact, the Fed raised interest rates in 1995 just to avoid future inflation, which was not in sight at the time. Since then the rate of inflation has declined. Some experts believe that currency depreciations in Asia could actually cause deflation in the United States, as import prices plunge. This is what happened in the 1930s and could happen again under similar circumstances. Thus deflation could occur in 1998; but once the dollar begins to collapse relative to other currencies, inflation could make a comeback in America, perhaps by the end of 1999.

Real Estate

Real estate and share prices normally move together. As stock markets continue to crash, land and house prices will decline all over the world, including Japan where land has already lost so much since 1990. However, Tokyo real estate is still very expensive, and is likely to fall some more.

Following Black Monday in October 1987, real estate suffered in many states in the United States. New York, California, Texas and Florida actually experienced major declines in house prices. The same is likely to happen in 1998 and 1999.

Bank CDs

The certificates of deposit in banks will be among the safest places to park your money, provided the deposits are insured.

Otherwise, government bonds and very large banks will be safe, because central banks will protect these investments. If there is one lesson to be learned from the 1930s, it is that banks should not be allowed to fail. If a government wants to stay in power today, it cannot afford to neglect its banking system.

A Silver Lining

However, all is not bleak in the future. There is a bright silver lining in an intensely cloudy picture. Every system in the past was better than the one it replaced. In fact, most eras of acquisitors were followed by a golden age. People were extremely happy after they got rid of the rule of acquisitors, and developed new economic, social, political and religious institutions.

Once money was no longer a dominant factor in politics, social discipline returned; technology improved further and real wages jumped; crime and pornography receded, and old-fashioned ethical and spiritual values made a comeback. People became more honest and compassionate after the darkness of acquisitive materialism vanished.

Several economic reforms were instituted that sharply reduced the concentration of income and wealth. The tax burden of the poor and the middle class declined. This has happened all through recorded history in every civilization, because this is the law of nature.

When the ruling elites become hard-hearted, corrupt and exploitative, then nature creates conditions to bring an end to their rule and to put a new class in power in accordance with the social cycle. The acquisitors' reign of greed takes society to such lows that a golden age must follow. There is no reason

166

why all of this will not occur again in the near future. After the downfall of the American business empire will come a global golden age. Such is the inevitable dictum of Sarkar's law of social cycles.

I have made some farfetched forecasts in the preceding pages. At this point you are entitled to know the odds of my being wrong. As mentioned before, in my earlier work I have listed 30 forecasts that I made between 1978 and 1995. For instance, in addition to predicting the fall of Soviet but not Chinese communism, I also foresaw the Iranian revolution of 1979, the extremely low inflation and interest rates of the 1990s, and so on. To my knowledge, I have missed two forecasts thus far. Therefore, the probability of a forecasting error on my part is 2 out of 30, or 7%. Just in case I have overlooked another one or two failed forecasts, then the likelihood of my error is about 15%.

A Strategy for Investment

It appears to me that we are now where the world was in 1928 or 1929. Great optimism overflowed at the time, with stock prices soaring and unemployment plunging. Few realized that our planet was on the brink of an economic collapse. How could any one even imagine that? After all, inflation was zero, the government bond rate was 4%, and joblessness was just 3% in the United States. But the world, then as now, was in the midst of a speculative bubble. Globally, debt was soaring, and competitive devaluations had begun.

Within a year the house of cards came tumbling down. What happened to South Korea at the end of 1997 occurred to the United States at the end of 1929. Can the unthinkable happen again? Of course, it can. Human nature has not changed for better. The greed factor is worse now than at that time. So is the speculative bubble.

1929 and the 1930s can easily repeat themselves for the whole world, and the odds of that happening are better than 60%. Under such circumstances, one has to be very careful with ones money. One ought to avoid all sorts of risky investments, such as stocks, bonds and real estate. Even the purchase of gold, which is a great hedge against uncertainty, is not that simple now because of an impending threat of deflation, in which prices actually fall.

Personally, I would be extremely cautious until the dust settles somewhat in 1999. If I owned any stocks and bonds, I would sell now, and park my money in certificates of deposit in different, not just one, banks, or in short term government bonds maturing in two years or less. The long term investment decisions can be made at the end of 1999 or beyond.

This is a riskless strategy for financial preparation. You may not like such extreme caution, especially at a time when the United States seems to be invincible in almost every area. But I am not a risk taker, especially when the handwriting is clearly written on the wall. In any case, no matter what you do, we are all heading toward an unprecedented golden age, which usually comes after some hard times.

* * *

7. Economic Reform

Just a few decades ago, we lived by the adage that if character is lost, everything is lost, if health is lost something is lost, but if money is lost, nothing is lost. Today, we believe exactly the opposite: if character is lost, nothing is lost, if health is lost, something is lost, but if money is lost, everything is lost. All over the world, the public, with very few exceptions, is obsessed with money and cares little for much else. A great degradation of moral values has occurred in just 50 years, and much of it has resulted from the cultural exports of the American business empire.

The empire has clearly outlived its usefulness. A new system has to replace capitalism and its materialistic way of life, if people want to lead ethical, compassionate and happy lives.

Capitalism has certainly taught the world how to meet the physical needs of a fast growing population. It has enriched our lives by creating machines that provide comforts only the royalty could afford in the past. Today, machines heat and cool our homes, mop our floors, do the cooking, and offer luxuries that a few decades back only an army of servants could provide.

Because of our single-minded devotion to things material, we have lost sight of the other aspects of our existence. In the process, morality has been shattered. People lead their lives constantly fearing for their personal safety. We need only open the newspapers to see the most horrendous kind of violence all around. Children are killing their parents, parents their children; students murder other students and teachers. The elderly are robbed and assaulted everyday.

We need a system that preserves the technological accomplishments of capitalism, while taking us back to old-fashioned virtues. We need to respect the dignity of human life; compassion and honesty must be rewarded; leaders must chase ethical principles, not money.

There is a great vacuum today in the realm of ideas: We need a new philosophy that reconciles our various needs without sacrificing the material gains we have made through new technology and rapid industrialization. P. R. Sarkar, the discoverer of the law of social cycles, has admirably filled this vacuum, and offered a new socio-economic system called Prout, which is designed to fulfil the crying needs of humanity today.

Prout stands for progressive utilization theory; that is" pro" from progressive, "u" from utilization and "t" from theory together make up Prout. The idea is that all our actions and institutions should be such as lead to human and social

170

progress.

Balance among Three Forces

Prout offers new ideas for all three aspects of our existence, namely the physical, the intellectual and the spiritual. True progress occurs only when a balance is maintained within each aspect and among all three of them. Our troubles have multiplied, because we have lost sight of this balance and are concerned with only the material side of life. How else do you explain the wild climb of European and US share prices in the last two months of 1997, even though stock and currency markets crumbled day after day in the fastest growing economies of Asia and Latin America. Driven, as always, by super greed, the business elites offered well-polished misinformation to the shareholders and kept their empire alive around the world.

Prout is a vast philosophy with many fertile branches. My concern here is only with Proutist economic reforms so as to stabilize the world economy. The United States and Japan are the two largest economies, and if they adopt the suggested reforms, it may still be possible to contain what is now being called the Asian contagion. We should do our best to avert the economic thunderbolt that is likely to strike the global share markets in the near future.

Real Wage and GDP

According to Prout, a vibrant or dynamic economy is one where the living standard rises for everybody. When improving technology makes the rich richer without bettering the lot of the poor and the middle class, the economy is essentially static and exploitative. The glitter of new gadgets, computers and autos then fades before the stagnant living standard of the masses.

After Bill Clinton became the US President in January 1993, GDP growth in America rose sharply. In the final quarter of 1994, the growth rate even exceeded 5%, the highest level in nearly a decade. American companies had introduced new technology at a fast pace. Yet the real wage declined for almost 75% of the workforce and the rate of poverty continued to rise.

Economists today call this sad phenomenon technological dynamism. Prout calls it exploitation. In fact, it is a diabolical monstrosity, reminiscent of medieval feudalism, where the fruit of back-breaking work by the serfs was extracted by the feudal landlord. The only difference is that now the fruit of rising national productivity, resulting from the increased use of computers, is extorted by business executives and company chairmen in the name of rising efficiency that is supposed to raise social welfare.

The poor and the middle class, husband and wife, strive day and night, master new technology, work up to 60 hours a week, and what do they get in return -- a declining real wage. Such is the tyranny of modern capitalism and the business elites that support it.

In order to determine the state of an economy, traditional economics examines the level and growth of real GDP, which is the production of all final goods and services valued at retail market prices. If the GDP, after adjustment for inflation, declines over two consecutive quarters, economists call it a recession. If the real GDP declines over several years, it becomes a depression.

Otherwise, the economy is alleged to be satisfactory,

172

especially if the growth of real GDP exceeds 3%. In this definition, for instance, Japan's recession was over in 1992. Never mind how the public and the employees feel. The government declared the recession over just because the real GDP no longer declined over two successive quarters.

Real GDP is an aggregated concept and it lumps together the incomes of the extremely wealthy with those of the very poor. In any economy, normally 5% of the public is affluent, 30% is poor and the rest belongs to the middle class. If the income of the top 5% soars, it is possible for the GDP to rise while the incomes of the other 95% decline or remain constant. Something like this has been happening in America since 1973 and has become worse since the election of Bill Clinton. The same thing has been happening in Japan since 1990.

In evaluating an economy, Prout examines the average real wage, which measures the purchasing power of people, i.e. the salary is adjusted for inflation. According to Prout, if real income falls for a majority of the public, then the economy is in recession, even if real GDP growth is high. The economy is in depression if the average real wage and employment fall or stay low for more than three years.

Prout's economy and concepts reflect common sense and how the general public feels. In this view, Japan has been in a recession since 1991. Even though real GDP has grown a bit, real income has declined for the vast majority of people because of a rise in unemployment, a sharp fall in overtime work and thousands of bankruptcies for small businessmen.

The United States has also been in recession since 1990 as the real wage has been decreasing for the vast majority of the population, in spite of respectable growth in GDP and productivity. In the traditional view, the Great Depression was over in 1933, even though US unemployment was at 17%

even as late as 1939.

Balanced Economy

Prout argues that in order to expand the living standard for everybody, countries should have a balanced economy. The foremost feature of such an economy is diversification as opposed to specialization.

It is well known that a prudent investor does not keep all his eggs in one basket, because if the basket were to fall, all the eggs could break at the same time. Instead, he diversifies by investing in a variety of assets or baskets. He buys stocks, bonds, real estate, gold and so on. By diversifying his portfolio of assets, a wise investor minimizes his risk. If one asset declines in value, the others could rise and trim his losses.

The Nikkei index has fallen severely since 1990; so have Japanese real estate prices; but long-term bonds have sharply gained. In Japan, those who had a diversified portfolio of stocks, bonds and real estate have not suffered as much as those who invested only in stocks and real estate. The idea behind a balanced economy is the same.

A diversified economy is far more stable and immune to the threat of speculative bubbles, market crashes, recessions and depressions than a specialized economy. Economic diversification occurs when a country allocates its resources to many important sectors. The main sectors are agriculture, forestry and fisheries, manufacturing, mining, construction (or housing), and a variety of services.

When a country meets most of its needs for food, manufactured goods, construction materials and services from its own production without dependence on foreign countries, then its economy is diversified or balanced.

174

For convenience, various sectors can be grouped into three categories, namely primary, secondary and tertiary. The primary sector includes agriculture, forestry, fisheries and mining; the secondary sector includes construction and manufacturing and the tertiary sector includes the remaining industries. In this classification, the primary sector has the lowest labor productivity, whereas the secondary sector has the highest productivity. When a nation meets most of its consumption needs from its own production, then its economy is diversified. This is the ideal case of diversification.

However, some nations lack raw materials. Japan, the little tigers and Germany fall into this category. Others have little fertile land. Saudi Arabia, Kuwait and the U.A.E. are a case in point. Such countries cannot have an adequate primary sector. In this case, a diversified economy may be defined as one that exports goods and services mostly to meet the needs of its primary goods.

By contrast, when a nation specializes in certain sectors and depends excessively on foreign markets for exports and imports, its economy is unbalanced. It puts most of its eggs in one basket and is vulnerable to outer shocks such as the ones generated recently by currency speculators. It is subject to recessions and depressions, as defined by Prout; that is to say, it may have high unemployment or its real wage may be stagnant or even decline, in spite of soaring labor productivity.

Prout favors a balanced economy because the post-war history of America, Japan, Canada and Australia shows that wage and productivity growth were higher when these nations were diversified, and growth slowly fell as their degree of specialization increased. It is true that the Asian tigers developed rapidly by following the track of specialization, but their high growth rates depended greatly on exports to diversified economies, which also invested heavily in Asia.

Economic history of the last two centuries reveals that economic diversification is vastly superior to export specialization.

Among various sectors of production, manufacturing, mining and construction have the highest productivity, whereas agriculture and services normally have the lowest productivity. The housing industry has a large production value, which is the same thing as productivity, because house prices tend to be high in any economy, especially where land is scarce. Similarly, in manufacturing also the production value tends to be large.

In mining, productivity is high in countries like Japan where raw materials are scarce, and low in countries like India where industrialization is low and raw materials relatively abundant. It may be added that productivity depends not only on improved technology but also on the product price. That is why expensive things like autos, appliances, etc. have high productivity.

In agriculture and services the production value tends to be small. This is because demand for food is limited by physical needs. How much extra rice or fish can you eat as your income rises? Not much. But there is no such limit for manufacturing. If you become rich, you can switch to higher priced cars, computers, and so on.

In services also the production value tends to be low, because it is difficult to constantly improve technology in service industries. The scope for raising productivity in restaurants, hotels, air lines, buses, railroads, insurance companies, banks, education, legal needs, retailing, etc. is rather limited. The production value in these areas lags behind that in construction and manufacturing, where productivity and

176

its growth tend to be far higher.

To sum up, construction and manufacturing have the highest production value, and services and agriculture the lowest, with mining somewhere in the middle.

A diversified economy is one which has a good mix of both high and low productivity industries, whereas a specialized economy has excessive amounts of some sectors and little of others. Among various areas, construction is essentially a non-traded industry; that is, it is very difficult to export or import finished houses, although construction materials, such as cement, bricks, lumber and pre-fabricated walls and structures can be moved from one country to another.

Nations can, of course, specialize or diversify in the other four areas -- manufacturing, mining, services and agriculture. Until 1970, most countries were diversified economies, but began to specialize increasingly thereafter. Canada and Australia specialized in mining and agriculture, the United States in agriculture and services, and Japan in manufacturing.

Thus Japan chose to specialize in the high productivity sector, whereas the United States, Canada and Australia focused on industries with lower production values. Not surprisingly, Japan continued to grow faster than other advanced economies. Real wages began to fall in Australia and the United States after 1973, whereas in Japan they rose a bit before taxes and were constant after taxes were deducted.

The moral of this whole argument is that specialization hurts the workers, even if a country focuses on high priced products. After the early 1970s, rising productivity failed to raise after-tax wages, even in Japan, while in North America and Australia, real wages fell in spite of rising productivity. In tiger economies, which preferred specialization in export sectors, growth was fast but wages rose very slowly. This is not Prout's idea of development.

Another argument in favor of diversification is the global competition for manufacturing. Since manufacturing tends to have higher production value than agriculture and services, all countries seek to have a piece of manufacturing. That is why the United States wants Japan to import US cars, even though American cars tend to be inferior. Now it is impossible for all countries to specialize in manufacturing. There is not enough global demand to support excessive production of manufactured goods in every country.

The auto industry is a case in point. In Japan the production capacity for cars is at 12 million autos per year. In the United States the total capacity is for 20 million cars. But the combined auto demand in the US and Japan is for only 22 million cars. There is then extra capacity for 10 million cars in the two countries. This is one reason for currently stagnant wages in both nations. This is also a huge waste of capital, which could have been productively used elsewhere.

In order to eliminate poverty from the world, it is necessary that, as far as possible, every country should produce some manufactured goods, which has a higher productivity and pays higher wages. The high wage sector then tends to create demand for high quality housing, as well as services. Thus vibrant manufacturing is needed to generate other vibrant industries.

Without adequate manufacturing an economy tends to stagnate, as low manufacturing means that the high wage sector is small. This tends to dampen the demand for housing and services as well. This way, real wages are low throughout the economy.

Thus, it is essential that, if at all feasible, every nation should produce as much manufacturing as it can to meet domestic needs. This should be done, even if its productivity and quality are not as high as those in other countries, because manufacturing is essential for a healthy economy.

The experience of the United States, Japan and Canada shows that their real wage growth was at its peak when about 25%-30% of their work force was employed in manufacturing. This happened until the early 1970s. In the late 1970s and the 1980s, the proportion of manufacturing employment fell sharply in Canada and America, whereas it rose a bit in Japan.

At present, just 16% of the labor force is employed in North American manufacturing, which is about where Canada and the US were in the 19th century. The North American continent has lost its dynamism and become a major source of labor's exploitation, where real wages for some service workers are below those prevailing before the First World War. Such has been the devastation of the industrial heartland in America and Canada since the early 1970s. This is what happens when manufacturing shrinks so much.

Australia is another sad story of the industrial breakdown; there less than 18% of the work force is now employed in manufacturing, which has been shrinking since 1974. No wonder its real wages have also been falling since that year. Australia has vast natural resources, so do Canada and the United States, but that has not prevented a decline in their real wages. Such are the effects of a falling employment share in manufacturing.

A diversified economy in today's high-tech age has about 30% of labor employed in manufacturing, another 8%-10% in construction, another 10% in mining and agriculture and the remaining 50% or more in services. These are, of course, approximations and they may vary a bit from economy to economy.

Japan has practically no mining industry and it imports much of its raw materials from abroad. Therefore, a large mining sector, as stated earlier, is not essential for a diversified or balanced economy, but its presence helps the nation in raising its living standard, as it once did in Canada, Australia and America. Germany is another case of a diversified economy, even though the mining industry is small there as well.

Supply And Demand

Economic diversification is only one feature of a balanced economy. Another feature is that domestic supply and demand are equal in most industries at affordable prices. Similarly, at the national level, supply and demand are close to each other. The idea is to emphasize the laws of markets. Few nations can suppress the markets for long. The Soviet Union tried to do it with disastrous effects for its economy.

An economy consists of many markets. There are markets not only for various goods, such as automobiles, electronics, furniture, appliances, etc., but also for resources, such as labor, land, capital, raw materials and credit or money. In addition, there are markets for stocks, bonds, futures, options and so on. Thus, there are markets for hundreds of things nowadays.

In a diversified economy where international trade plays a minor role, domestic supply and demand for most goods should be close to each other at affordable prices. The price affordability is important here because, in theory, every market can be in balance at some exorbitantly high price. In addition, demand and supply always appear to be equal to the amount of goods exchanged. If one hundred houses are sold, then demand and supply must be equal to one hundred. In this sense, supply

180

and demand are equal by definition to the quantity exchanged.

How can then supply and demand ever differ? They are certainly equal at some price, but at all other prices they will be unequal. Suppose Sony sharply reduces the price of its TVs without increasing its production. At that low price there is great demand for Sony TVs and not enough supply. In this case, demand exceeds supply at the lower price. Thus, the supply-demand balance always refers to a certain price. If the balancing price is generally affordable, we say that the supply and demand are in equilibrium in a market; but not otherwise.

Take, for instance, the land market in Japan during the 1980s, when the demand for land far exceeded its supply. As a result, the demand for land equalled its supply at an unbelievably high price. Clearly, the land market was unbalanced at that time, because the resulting market price was far away from normal. The same was true for the stock market as the Nikkei index of share prices rose above 38,000 at the end of 1989. Demand for stocks then far exceeded their supply, so that stock prices kept rising. These prices were too high to be affordable to the general public. Clearly, the stock market was then in imbalance.

In a balanced economy, supply and demand for various goods equal each other at prices close to the recent average. If the market-clearing price that equates supply with demand is far above the recent average, then that market is unbalanced. European and US stock exchanges are clearly out of balance today.

Similarly, the market-clearing price should not be too far below the recent average. Take, for instance, the labor market. Here, the demand for labor comes from companies and the supply from households and workers. The price in this market is the real wage, i.e. the inflation-adjusted salary, including the bonus.

If there is unemployment in the economy, then labor demand is less than labor supply at the prevailing real wage. If the real wage falls, labor demand will rise as the employers are then willing and able to hire more workers. At the same time, some people will be discouraged by lower wages and drop out of the employment market. As the real wage continues to fall, labor supply will fall to the level of rising labor demand, and unemployment will be eliminated. Will this market then be in balance? Not necessarily.

If the real wage falls sharply below the recent average, then the supply and demand for labor will be equal only because of so many discouraged workers who quit the labor force. And if the real wage falls in spite of rising productivity, then clearly this market is in imbalance, because common sense dictates that a person should earn more as he becomes more productive. So if he earns less, then evidently there is something wrong. The laws of economics must all conform with common sense.

There are two types of goods -- traded and non-traded goods. Normally, goods and services that cannot be physically moved cannot enter into foreign trade. Land, houses, education, etc. are non-traded goods. Most other products can be exported or imported. They are called traded goods and services.

For non-traded goods market balance occurs when domestic supply and demand are equal at an affordable price, which is close to the recent average price. For traded goods, by contrast, domestic demand differs from domestic supply at the price determined in the world market. For an exported good, domestic supply exceeds local demand, so that the surplus is exported. For an imported product, the local supply is less

182

than local demand, so that the excess demand is met by imports.

In the United States, the local supply of oil is much less than local demand. Therefore, the difference is imported from abroad. On the other hand, the domestic demand for airplanes is less than their production. Hence, the surplus planes are exported.

However, at the national level, the supply and demand for all goods and services are equal in a balanced economy. In a totally self-sufficient economy with no trade, national supply and demand are always equal. When trade exists, domestic demand and supply are different for some industries, but even then national supply and demand are equal in a balanced economy.

National demand is the total spending on goods and services by consumers, businesses and the government. National supply, on the other hand, is the GDP. Therefore, economic balance requires that GDP equals national demand or spending. When spending and production are equal at the national level, the country's trade is in balance, i.e. its exports are no less or greater than its imports.

Thus, a balanced economy also has balanced trade; in other words, it has neither a trade deficit nor a trade surplus in the current account. In reality, exports and imports can rarely be exactly equal. In that case, balanced trade means that exports and imports are close to each other, so that the trade deficit or surplus is small.

Other Features

When economic development occurs, the environment should not suffer in the process. If it does, then economic growth is not progressive in Sarkar's definition, for a positive movement on the growth front has been accompanied by a negative movement in the quality of the environment. A balanced economy maintains a balanced environment as well. What is the point in enjoying the comfort of modern conveniences while suffering from the dreaded diseases of a polluted atmosphere? Rising production alone cannot be called growth if air becomes unbreathable and water becomes undrinkable.

Another feature of a balanced economy is that it has no budget deficits; furthermore, its financial institutions, especially banks, are tightly regulated, so that speculation in asset markets is limited. Similarly, stock markets offer vehicles only for business investment but not for gambling. In other words, a balanced economy does not permit loans for any kind of speculation.

America and Japan: 1950-1997

Both the United States and Japan had somewhat balanced economies from 1950 to 1970, but since then their economies have become greatly unbalanced In the first period, they had nearly balanced trade and balanced budgets. Foreign trade, especially in America, was small relative to other sectors. Banks were tightly regulated to keep interest rates affordable for housing. Share markets and business mergers were also restrained to keep them away from wild speculation.

In these circumstances, both countries enjoyed a fast rise in living standards, as real wages rose in proportion to productivity for the vast majority of workers. However in the early 1970s, under the influence of economists and politicians hired by the top executives of rich corporations, economic policies changed. Gradually, budgets went into deficits, and

184

trade became unbalanced: Japan began to develop a surplus and the United States a deficit in the balance of payment. Furthermore, banks and other financial institutions were deregulated.

As policies changed in the second period, speculation grew; real wages stagnated in Japan and fell in America, while corporate profits and executives' earnings soared. Stagnant wages created the need for two-earner families, with both husband and wife working to earn a comfortable living. As a result, children were neglected; parents had little time to educate them into moral values. Social degeneration had to occur.

In the United States, the tax burden was transferred from the rich to the rest. Thus after-tax real wages fell even more, and the rich got richer. In other words, when economies were balanced, everyone prospered; but when they became unbalanced because of rising trade, financial deregulation and speculation, the living standard fell or stagnated for the vast majority of people in both America and Japan, even though productivity continued to rise.

At the end of 1997, both nations had become giant casinos, where gamblers throw away their money for quick but illusory gains. In fact, virtually, the whole world had become a mammoth casino.

Economic Reforms

In order to stabilize the global economy and restore prosperity, every country should adopt Proutist policies that create a balanced economy. The following measures are urgently needed:

* * *

1. *Housing Tax Credit*

The main problem in Japan and some tiger economies is insufficient demand, which forces them to send their production to foreign countries, which then have to accept huge trade deficits. At this point, trade imbalances are destabilizing Europe and the United States.

Rising domestic demand in Asia will solve many problems in the world. One of the best ways to stimulate demand is to promote the housing industry. This is because when people buy new homes they also buy refrigerators, washers, dryers, furniture, carpets, vacuum cleaners, paintings, antiques and so on. Therefore new homes and apartments should be made attractive and affordable to the public.

The US government in the past has offered housing tax credits to fight severe recessions with great success. High consumption in America results chiefly from the availability of affordable housing. According to the Housing Loan Corporation of Japan, home owners spend five times as much money on appliances in the first year of home purchase as the average worker. Even though house prices continue to fall in Japan, they are still too high for most people, especially as they lack confidence in the economy.

Suppose the government were to offer an income tax credit of 10% on the purchase of a new house, not an old one, over the three years between 1998 to 2000. Let us say the cost of a new home is $100,000; 10% of this figure is $10,000. That is then the tax saving to a new home owner against his income tax bill. At the end of the year the proud buyer of a new house can present his receipt to the government and claim his tax refund. All the tiger economies should also adopt this policy to stimulate home demand.

186

In Japan and Korea where land is scarce, the government should build high-rise apartments with a large square footage and then sell them to the public. Big residences are not only comfortable, they also greatly increase consumer spending. Hong Kong and Singapore have done this with great success, and other Asian countries should follow their example.

2. Reducing Housing Costs

For home owners with negative equities, i.e. those whose mortgages now exceed the market value of their house, the government should make an offer to refinance their loans at low long term interest rates. This would sharply reduce their monthly mortgage payments. Thailand, Indonesia, Korea, Hong Kong and Japan face this problem, because real estate prices have fallen in the current slump.

On the supply side of real estate, an all out effort should be made to increase the supply of residential land and bring its price down. Land prices have fallen sharply in Japan since 1990, but they had risen from an index of 55 in 1950 to 21,000 in 1991. Even if the index falls to 10,000 or even 5,000, the land price will still be extremely high.

All regulations and capital gains taxes that hinder the sale of land for building homes should be eliminated. At the same time, the government capital budget should be directed towards increasing the supply of habitable areas through reclamation. This may be done by blasting the hills and constructing offshore islands, such as the 1,200 hectare area on which Kansai International Airport was built. Future industry may be located on man-made islands.

Much of the population in Japan is concentrated in Tokyo, Osaka, Nagoya and Kyoto. In order to relieve congestion and

187

bring land prices down in the largest cities, businesses should be given tax incentives to re-locate industry. Hokkaido in the north and Kyushu in the south are under-populated. Industries should be given tax incentives for re-location away from congested cities. This will also lower the average price of land.

3. *Tight Banking Regulation*

The banking industry should be tightly regulated every where. We should remember the lessons of the 1920s, when deregulation of the financial sectors created a speculative bubble, which then burst open and plunged the world into a catastrophic depression. Regulations on banking and stock markets were then introduced in the 1930s, but were gradually removed after the 1970s. The regulations of the 1930s should be readopted.

The fever of deregulation is rising in Japan nowadays. Some experts believe that if various sectors of the economy are deregulated, everything will be fine. Imports will rise, consumer prices will fall, the economy will become efficient, productivity will go up, and consumers will be happy.

This is the same type of hope that the economists have been offering to Americans for the past two decades. Yes, imports have risen, inflation has fallen, people are more efficient through the increasing use of computers, and productivity has risen slightly. All this has happened as free traders had hoped, and only one part of their argument has not materialized. Consumers are unhappy with their incomes. The prices they face have gone up very slowly, but their salaries have hardly moved. Consumers are unhappy because their pre-tax and after-tax real wages have both declined massively, in spite of rising productivity.

Deregulation of industry, not the financial sector, is always desirable, but its gains come only in the long run. Today, nations need immediate help; they need short -term policies. The world's most famous economist, John Maynard Keynes used to say, "In the long run we are all dead." Everyone is a worker first and a consumer next. An unhappy employee cannot be a happy consumer. Free traders do not understand this. Nor do they realize that shrinking home manufacturing means shrinking real wages for the vast majority of the people.

Deregulation should be introduced in Japan to enhance domestic competition in all industries, but not to encourage imports of manufactured goods. Furthermore, the financial sector, as stated earlier, should never be deregulated, because that creates speculative waves, which later bring a lot of pain in the form of high unemployment and debts. We should realize that other economic policies are urgently needed to resolve short-term problems.

4. *Replacing Social Security Taxes with Tariffs*

Social Security taxes or fees are among the biggest destroyers of employment and wages. Their burden falls heavily on the poor and small businessmen. They should be cut and, if possible, eliminated. The resulting loss of revenue should be made up with new tariffs on imports. The problem is especially serious in Europe, especially Italy, France and Germany. As a result, these nations have very high unemployment. Tariffs should replace the social insurance fees.

The consumer will have to pay higher prices, but his tax burden will fall by the same amount. Therefore, the consumer will neither be hurt nor benefit from this policy. But employment will rise, production will occur where demand is, and international trade will fall. The economies will be less dependent on each other, and the follies of other countries will not hurt the nation itself. Furthermore, the environmental quality will greatly improve. International trade and the resulting transportation of goods using oil are among the biggest creators of pollution. Tax and tariff policies should be friendly to the environment, especially when production is not affected.

When tariffs replace Social Security fees, the total tax burden and revenue will be unchanged Only trade will fall, and production will be located near demand centers. Output of the world economy will not suffer. Employment will rise as labor costs decline from reduced Social Security levies. However, the tariff reform is a long term measure and should be undertaken only after the supply demand gap in the world has disappeared.

5. *Free Foreign Investment*

Prout is against free foreign trade, but it favors free foreign investment. All barriers against the inflow of overseas capital into home industries should be removed, so that maximum production occurs where demand is maximum.

6. *Eliminating Speculation*

All forms of speculation should be outlawed. This means that banks should be permitted to lend money only for consumption and business investment, but not for the purchase of stocks, business mergers and property not intended for

190

personal use.

7. *Progressive Taxation*

As much as possible, the tax system should be made progressive in every nation. In other words, the wealthy should pay a larger percentage of their income than the poor after all taxes are taken into account. This will raise consumer demand around the globe and thus lower the demand-supply gap.

These then are the reforms that are urgently needed to stabilize the world economy and restore its prosperity. I have analyzed them briefly here, because a detailed discussion is available in my two books, *The Great American Deception*, and *Japan: The Return to Prosperity*. Once the Proutist reforms suggested above are adopted, the world will move toward a golden age. This is the dictate of the law of social cycles, which has never failed in 5000 years of recorded history.

The news from Japan and other lands in Asia is grim nowadays. If Indonesia's forest fires don't cause you much anxiety, then the constant stream of business closings does. There is little from there to cheer us today. All is not lost, however. Great economic and social systems are born only when the human spirit has reached the bottom of despair. The dawn comes inevitably after the night becomes the darkest. Japan, the land of the rising sun, knows this very well.

The deepening crisis of today will prove to be a blessing in disguise, because it will force a reevaluation of our economic policies and our materialistic way of life. It will pave the way for the emergence of Prout that will solve most of our

191

problems pertaining to the three aspects of life, the physical, the intellectual and the spiritual. But the first step in establishing the new system is to cure the economic crisis, and that is what I have stressed in this book. My one life-time goal as an economist has been to abolish poverty from the world, and I need your heartiest support to achieve this goal. Let's create a better life for our children.

In Asia, people are worried by a specter of joblessness and poverty, whereas the rest of the world is plagued by violent crime, which results from super materialism. At places the problem is the lack of money, at others, it is the abundance of money in a few hands. Most of these troubles will be cured in the near future.

Come, my sisters and brothers, come; do not despair. You have no time to lose. Join the forward march of Prout to usher a new age in our greed-scarred world. You will be the harbingers of a new universalistic philosophy. From you will sprout a life-giving movement, choking poverty, super materialism, and misery from the world. The challenge is formidable, and the hurdles vast. Pay no heed. Rise, and sing with me the immortal song that captures the Proutist spirit.

> The bigger the goal, the bigger the obstacle
> The bigger the obstacle, the bigger the achievement
> So blame the failure not on the obstacle
> But on the absence of relentless effort.

To know more about Prout, call Proutist Universal in Washington DC at 202-829-2278.

Appendix to Chapter 4

The Appendix contains some of the figures that were discussed but not displayed in the main body of the text. These figures offer visual confirmation of the global speculative bubble explored in Chapter 4. Some figures use stock price data in terms of both the US dollar and the local currency, whereas, for countries with a relatively restrained level of inflation, the underlying data are in terms of the local currency only.

Figure A.1

Stock-Price Index In Chile: 1987-96

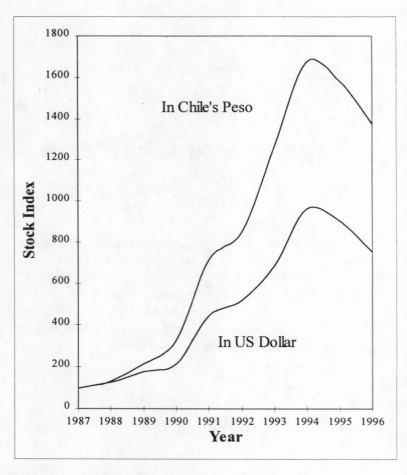

In Chile's Peso

In US Dollar

Source: Morgan Stanley Capital International

Figure A.2

Stock-Price Index In India: 1992-96

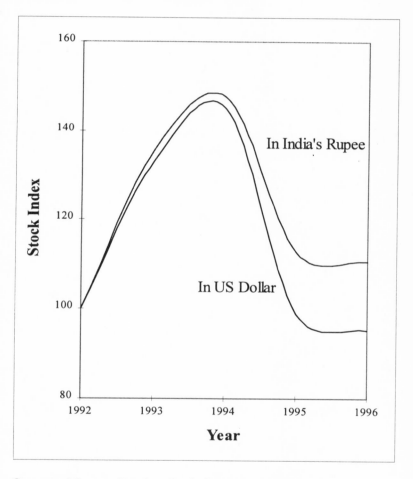

Source: Morgan Stanley Capital International

Figure A.3

Stock-Price Index In Indonesia: 1987-96

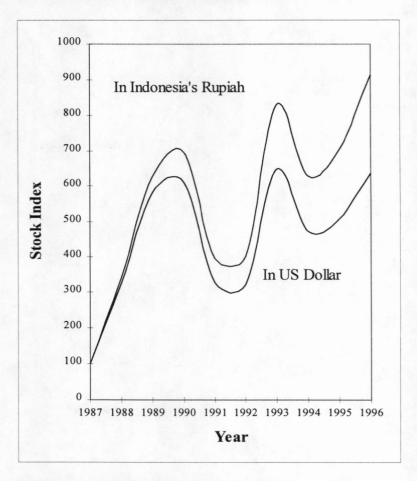

Source: Morgan Stanley Capital International

Figure A.4

Stock-Price Index In Malaysia: 1987-96

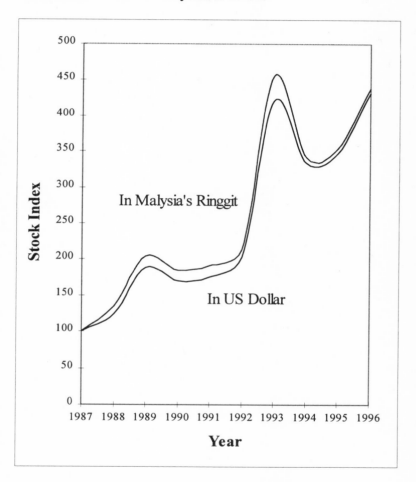

Source: Morgan Stanley Capital International

Figure A.5

Stock-Price Index In Mexico: 1987-96

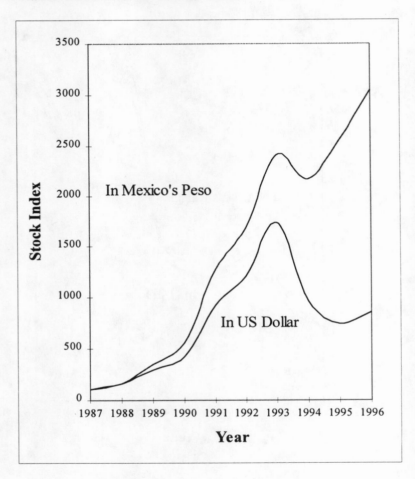

Source: Morgan Stanley Capital International

Figure A.6

Stock-Price Index In The Philippines: 1987-96

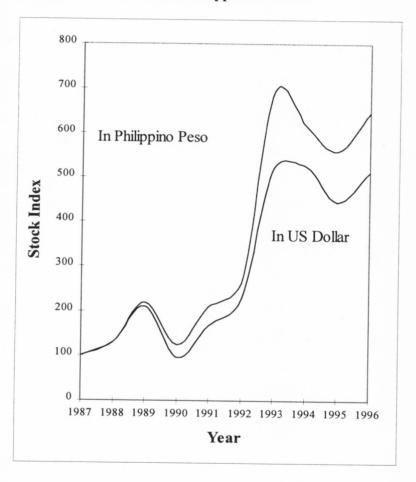

Source: Morgan Stanley Capital International

Figure A.7

Stock-Price Index In Thailand: 1987-96

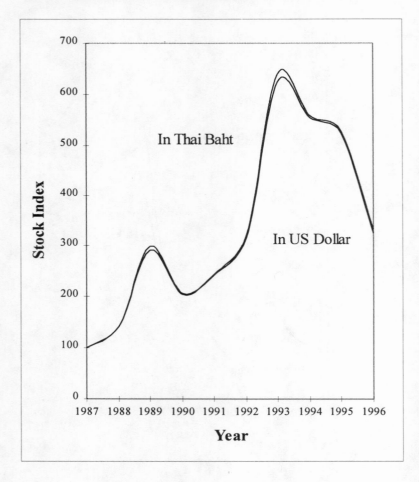

Source: Morgan Stanley Capital International

Figure A.8

Stock-Price Index In Venezuela: 1992-96

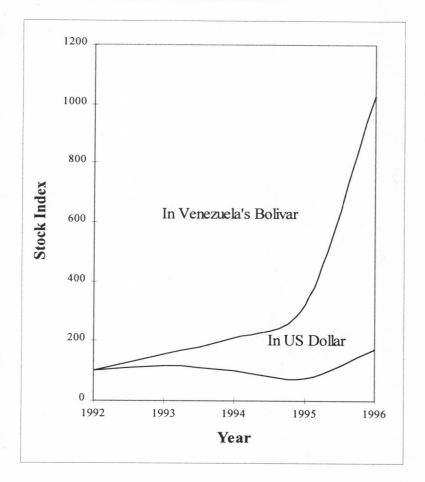

Source: Morgan Stanley Capital International

Figure A.9

Stock-Price Index In Australia: 1987-96

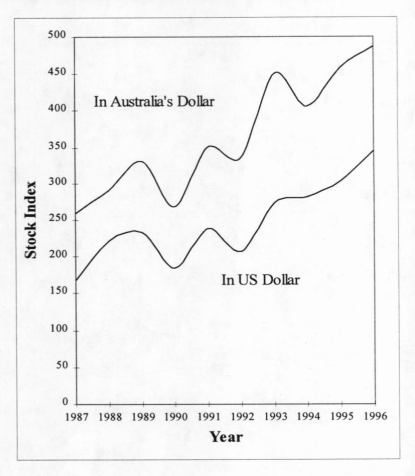

Source: Morgan Stanley Capital International

Figure A.10

Stock-Price Index In Canada: 1987-96

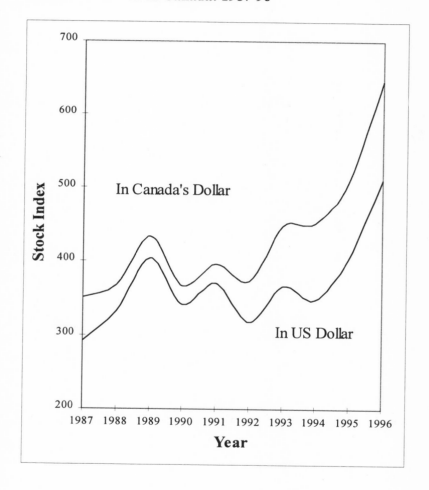

Source: Morgan Stanley Capital International

Figure A.11

Stock-Price Index In Italy: 1987-96

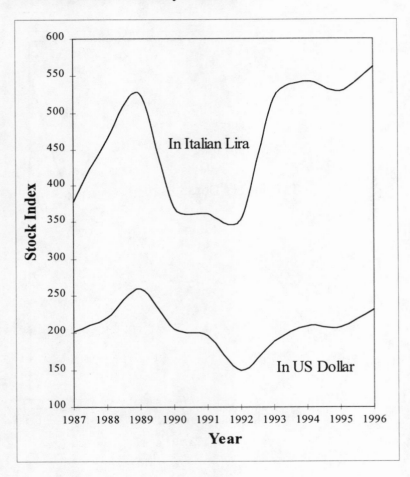

Source: Morgan Stanley Capital International

Figure 12

Stock-Price Index In Sweden: 1987-96

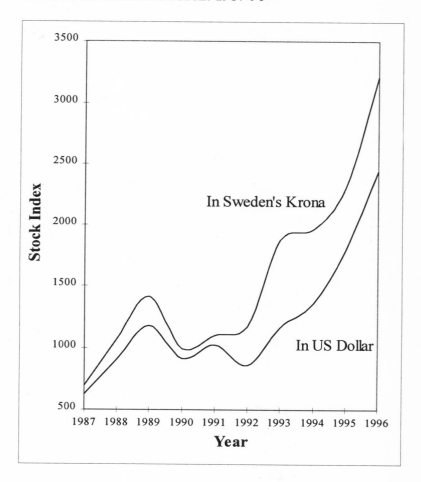

Source: Morgan Stanley Capital International

* * *

References

I have consulted the following books and articles in producing this work.

1. Ravi Batra, *The Great American Deception*, John Wiley and Sons, New York, 1996.
2. Ravi Batra, *Japan: The Return to Prosperity*, Sogo Horei, Tokyo, 1996.
3. Ravi Batra, *The Downfall of Capitalism and Communism*, Macmillan 1978 and Tokuma, 1995.
4. C. Chow, and M. Kellman, *Trade--the Engine of Growth*, Oxford University Press, New York, 1993.
5. Takatoshi Ito, *The Japanese Economy*, MIT Press, 1992.
6. Charles Kindleberger, *The World in Depression: 1929-1939*, University of California Press, 1986.
7. Leipziger, D. *Lessons from East Asia*, University of Michigan Press, Ann Arbor, 1997.
8. T. Lin, and C. Tuan, *The Asian Nies: Success and Challenge*, Lo Fung Learned Society, Hong Kong, 1993.
9. Ryoshin Minami, *The Economic Development Of Japan*, 2nd Edition, Macmillan, 1994.
10. Takafusa Nakamura, *The Postwar Japanese Economy*, 2nd Edition, Tokyo University Press, 1995.
11. P.S. Pierce, *The Dow Jones Averages: 1885-1990*, Mcgraw Hill, New York, 1995.
12. M. Rostovtzeff, A History of the Ancient World, Oxford University Press, London, 1926.
13. T. Saler, *All about Global Investing*, John Wiley & Sons, New York, 1996.
14. P. R. Sarkar, *Prout in a Nutshell, 1-20*, Orient Press, Calcutta, 1988.
15. A. So and S. Chiu, *East Asia and the World Economy,* Sage Publications, Thousand Oaks, 1995.
16. Ryuichiro Tachi, *The Contemporary Japanese Economy*, Tokyo University Press, 1993.

17. Kurokawa Toshio, "Problems Of The Japanese Working Class In Historical Perspective," in Tessa Morris-Suzuki and Siyama Takuro, Editors, *Japanese Capitalism Since 1945,* M.E. Sharpe, 1990.
18. Christopher Wood, *The Bubble Economy,* Atlantic Monthly Press, Atlanta, 1992
19. Christopher Wood, *The End Of Japan, Inc.,* Simon and Schuster, 1994.
20. John Woronoff, *The Japanese Economic Crisis,* Macmillan, 1992.
21. *Japan Statistical Yearbook,* 1996.
22. *Economic Statistics Annual,* 1995.
23. *Japan Almanac,* 1996.
24. *New York Times,* October 28, 1997, and November 24, 27, and 29, 1997.
25. *Time,* November 3 and 10, 1997.
26. *Wall Street Journal,* November 14, 1997.
27. *Economic Report of the President,* 1997, Department of Commerce, Washington, DC.
28. *Statistical Abstract of the United States,* 1997, Department of Commerce, Washington DC.
29. *International Financial Statistics: Yearbook,* International Monetary Fund, Washington DC.
30. *World Development Report,* 1991 and 1997, The World Bank, Washington DC.

* * *

Index

Order Form

We hope that this work has offered you a good deal of valuable information. If it has convinced you that an economic crisis is likely in 1998 and 1999, then you may consider presenting copies of this book to your relatives and friends. It could turn out to be your best gift to them. Here is how to order this and other thought provoking books by Ravi Batra.

1. Please send _____ copies of
   Stock Market Crashes of 1998-99. Price $ 25.00(Hardcov.)
   $20.00(paper bk.)

2. Please send _____ copies of
   The Downfall of Capitalism and Communism,
   Price $25.00
   (Hardcover)

Prices include postage and handling.

Name_____

Address_____

_____

City/State/Zip_____

Please make your check payable to Liberty Press, 2355 Trellis Place, Richardson, TX. 75081, USA, or call 1-800-248-4303.